LEGEND

of the

MONK

and the MERCHANT

Twelve Keys to Successful Living

TERRY FELBER

FOREWORD *by* Dave Ramsey

W PUBLISHING GROUP

AN IMPRINT OF THOMAS NELSON

ISBN 978-1-4003-3965-5 (TP)
ISBN 978-0-8499-4852-7 (HC)

DEDICATION

To my wife and best friend, Linda, and to my loving,
wonderful children Lia, Kristi, and David, who continue
to join with me in our family mission: loving God, loving
people; serving God, serving people.

Acknowledgments

I want to thank my good friends John Bolin, who collaborated with me on the writing and research of this book, and Steve Hickey, who helped with the study guide. Both continue to be a blessing in my life.

CONTENTS

Contents

FOREWORD

A mong Christians in North America today, I've noticed a tendency to err in one of two extremes when it comes to the believer's success in business. The first error is that wealth is evil, and if I work hard and, as a result, build some personal wealth, then I'm somehow evil too. It doesn't matter how I built that wealth. It doesn't matter what I choose to do with that wealth. All that matters is that wealth—financial success in business or at home—is morally wrong.

The second error is that wealth is somehow an indicator of God's blessing or favor. That is, God wants all His children to be filthy rich, and if you're not wealthy, it's the result of a weak faith. I firmly believe that both of these viewpoints are not only incorrect, but actually toxic to the Christian's view of business.

The problem with these perspectives is that neither is biblical. Both of these viewpoints make some assumptions about wealth that aren't found in Scripture at all. In fact, I think they're tied to a *pagan* belief that material possessions are inherently evil. But I've never read that in the Bible. I've always found Scripture to be more concerned with our heart and actions and beliefs around wealth than the actual possessions themselves. From a biblical standpoint, wealth and business success are amoral—*without morals*. "Things" are just tools to be used however we choose. So I can be evil with my wealth, or I can be generous with my wealth. It's not about the money; it's about what I choose to do with it.

As a business owner—as a *successful* business owner—this whole discussion is a big deal to me. I've always believed, much like Bob Briner discusses in his book *Roaring Lambs*, that Christians have a responsibility in business. We should actively take possession of segments of the marketplace for Christ instead of surrendering them to the other side. We don't claim the church as God's turf and surrender the marketplace as Satan's. We're alive, active, and moving in both, and I believe God puts a call on our lives to redeem the business world for His glory. That's been my goal my entire career.

During a time when I was really working through what I believed about all this, one of my team members gave me a book entitled *The Legend of the Monk and the Merchant*. God always has a way of giving us exactly what we need when we need it, right? I absolutely fell in love with this little book. It painted an incredible picture of exactly what I was working through, perfectly framing the debate in a way I could really get my arms around.

Author Terry Felber helped me put the whole church/business debate in a new light. I was finally able to express that the monk is holy—*and so is the merchant!* What the merchant does *is a ministry*. Everything we do as believers can and should be done from a paradigm of ministry. We're not called to separate our spiritual life from our work life, and we're not called to divide our Sunday morning worship from our Monday morning staff meetings. God is in both, and He blesses both.

I believe in this idea so strongly that I immediately ordered a big box of these books and made it required reading for my whole team. Since then, every single person we've hired has been required to read this book in their first ninety days with the company. That's not just because I think this is a "good read." It's because this book really outlines who we are and how we view our role in the marketplace. If we hire someone in our shipping department, they aren't just packing books into boxes; they're sending out messages of hope and encouragement to someone who needs a hand. If we hire someone to work in our customer care center, they aren't just answering the phone and reading a script; they're touching lives and giving a word of peace to someone in the middle of a storm. Everyone in the building knows that they're operating under a high calling, *because our work is holy*. No one here doubts that.

When we, as the people of God, view something as unholy, we start to see it with some level of disdain. I'm afraid that business has gotten that reputation in America today, but it's time for us to change how people *inside and outside* the church see American business. As you read this book, my goal for you is that you start to experience a paradigm shift, that you'll come to view everything you do in the marketplace as an act of holiness that will forever change the way you do business.

My team and I love this book, and I pray you enjoy it as much as we do.

—DAVE RAMSEY

CHAPTER ONE

THE STEPS OF
THE CATHEDRAL

Antonio strained to control the horse as they turned the corner and headed west in the direction of Rome. He glanced over his shoulder to see his grandson, Julio, asleep on a pile of straw in the small rear compartment of the cart. Even though it was the best horse and cart money could buy, they had been traveling for more than two days now, and Julio was beginning to feel it. Truthfully, they were both beginning to feel it. But Antonio didn't mind. He knew that the next few hours would change his grandson forever.

Antonio was nearly fifty-five, but appeared no older than forty-five. He was five feet eight, with long, gray hair and a neatly combed beard that fell cleanly in a sharp angle under his chin. The many days spent on the water and under the sun had tanned his face and highlighted his pale blue eyes. It was clear that Antonio was a man of wealth. His beautifully carved wagon seemed almost out of place in the rural countryside. He wore a cloak that was made from fine wool and lined with red silk imported from China. Around his neck hung a gold cross, and he wore an ornate hat that bore the markings of a distinguished lord. Antonio pulled his cloak over his face as a morning breeze swept across the countryside. The smell of spring flowers filling the air, he breathed deeply. A smile crossed his face as he thought of Julio, fast asleep behind him.

A sudden bump in the road, no doubt the result of the persistent spring rains, jolted Julio to his knees. Another hole sent him face-forward in the hay with a dull thud. "We're almost there, Julio," Antonio shouted back, ignoring the jostling and bumping behind him. A moment later, he felt a hand on his back as young Julio lumbered over the seat and took his place next to his grandfather.

"How much farther?" Julio asked as he attempted to regain his balance.

Antonio pulled the reins to avoid a peasant struggling with a load of wood. "It's just around that next corner." The woman quickly shuffled across the road as the cart passed by. Small buildings and better roads were now appearing on both sides of them, and Julio knew that these were the signs of city life. The scattered structures were soon replaced by larger buildings and ancient ruins. The glory of Rome slowly appeared in front of Julio's eyes. He scanned both sides of the street, looking for the great cathedral.

"Grandfather, how will I know which one it is?" Julio asked.

"Don't worry. You'll know."

The first signs were the massive pillars surrounding a grand plaza. Julio's mouth dropped open, and Antonio turned and smiled. The pillars appeared at least fifty feet high with colonnades towering above them. The white stone sparkled in the morning sun. As they drew closer, Julio could see the ornate stone carvings that adorned the huge structures.

"Welcome to St. Peter's," Antonio said as he pulled back tightly on the reins.

Julio lurched forward as the horse came to a stop, but he never said a word. His eyes were glued to the colonnades in front of him. As they approached the pillars and arches surrounding a great plaza, two Vatican guards recognized Antonio. Although people were not being allowed onto the plaza, the men gestured Antonio and Julio to pass into the main area leading to the cathedral. Julio gazed up at the great dome that formed the centerpiece to St. Peter's. He had never seen anything like it. His heart began to race. *How was this ever built?* he thought to himself.

As they walked through the front entry and into the main building, Julio couldn't keep himself from looking up. They were the only visitors allowed into the church today. Julio suddenly tugged at Antonio's sleeve and pointed to a wood scaffolding that rose upward toward a massive dome over a hundred feet high in the center of the main hallway. Lying across a crude board was a man staring directly ahead. The man on the board was frozen still, and for a moment Julio was sure he was asleep. "What's that man doing up there?" Julio asked.

"That's the master," whispered Antonio.

"Who?" Julio replied.

"Michelangelo."

Almost as quickly as he said the name, the man on the scaffold leaned over and waved slowly at the two visitors. In awe, Julio returned the greeting.

Julio was eighteen years old and taller than his grandfather. His deep blue eyes darted back and forth across the massive cathedral. He could hardly take in all the beauty of the place. They kept walking . . . and looking. Julio noticed several beautifully carved statues and immediately recognized them as Bible heroes. The cathedral was eerily silent as they moved across the floor. The sound of Julio's sandals slapping on the stone seemed to echo in every direction. Julio remembered how he had resisted when his mother had told him to wear the long cloak for this trip. Now he felt suddenly appropriate in his gray coat. He seemed like a monk from one of the nearby monasteries.

Antonio was moving quickly ahead of him, and Julio sped up his stride to catch him. They moved toward the front of the church. Directly before them was the main altar, surrounded by huge golden pillars that spiraled upward. The entire front of the cathedral seemed to be laced in gold. The colors of the mosaics and the stained glass bounced off the white marble floor and reflected in rainbow prisms across the massive room. Julio found himself lost in the beauty of the cathedral, and for a moment he was lost in time.

Suddenly, Julio heard the sound of people in the distance. A young monk had approached Antonio and was talking and pointing toward a hallway to the left. Antonio told his grandson that since the main church was still being painted and was not open to the public yet, a temporary chapel was being used for the morning mass. People were being allowed to enter the side chapel through an entrance on the east side of the building. The young monk led the way into another room, still larger than any church Julio had ever been in, and pointed them toward a stone bench in the back of the already-packed room. As the priests walked by, slowly waving their censers in worship, Julio couldn't help but stare as the smoke curled up toward God and the cavernous domes above them. His grandfather had told him so much about the cathedral, but now he was actually seeing it for himself. It was even more magnificent than he'd imagined. This trip to Rome had been shrouded in mystery from the beginning, and now Julio was beginning to wonder what else he would discover.

Nearly an hour had passed since the end of the mass. Neither one of them had said anything for a long time. They simply sat near the back of the chapel, gazing at the ornate walls and the endless arches and the beautiful stained glass. *How did all this ever come to be?* he thought to himself again. *How could anyone ever afford to build such a grand cathedral?* It was all too incredible to take in. Then, in silence and almost in unison, they stood and began to walk back toward the grand entrance and into the brilliance of the Vatican sun.

His grandfather had told him earlier that he had a special story to tell him and a great secret to reveal. And even though Julio had prodded and begged, he was told that he'd only hear it after they had worshiped at St. Peter's. Antonio slowed in front of the cathedral, still in the shade of the massive arches and pillars near the entrance. Julio nearly leapt toward his grandfather, now seated on a marble step, and settled himself onto the stone just a few feet away.

"Is it time, Grandfather?"

"Yes, Julio, it's time."

CHAPTER TWO

The MERCHANT of VENICE

It was late morning and the sun had settled high above the dome of St. Peter's. A slight breeze from somewhere beyond the plaza made the morning as idyllic as any Antonio could remember. He had been waiting several years for the opportunity to pass down to young Julio the principles that had made him successful. At eighteen, Julio was beginning to look more and more like his father, Valentino.

Julio had been born and raised in Venice with his four siblings, all girls. As the oldest, he was now expected to join in business with his father, who had become a well-known shipping merchant. A natural with numbers, Julio was placed under special tutelage at fourteen. Valentino had himself taken this same trek with Antonio some twenty years earlier and was glad when it was suggested that it was now Julio's time.

"Tell me, Grandfather. Tell me the story. I'm ready," Julio proclaimed in a cool tone, trying desperately to hide his excitement.

"I suppose the best place to start is at the monastery."

"The monastery?" questioned Julio.

"Yes. I was raised in a small monastery on the outskirts of Venice. I can still hear the sounds of the monks as they chanted together during their early morning prayers. I remember the way that Felipo, my father, would lift me into the air as a child and spin me in a circle. He always said it was to get me closer to God," grinned Antonio.

"But, Grandfather, I thought you were adopted." Julio

hadn't budged from his place on the cathedral steps, and his eyes were fixed on Antonio's. It was as though he was recording every word in his heart.

"Yes, I was. But I considered Felipo my father. After all, he was the only father that I had ever known. In fact, it had never really occurred to me that I was adopted at all. Since before I could remember, I'd lived at the monastery. I was very young when your great-grandparents died, and as far as I was concerned the monastery was my home."

"Grandfather, what happened to your mother and father?" He wondered if he should ask. But knowing the full story was too much of a temptation.

Antonio took a deep breath and then began.

"The story has been told to me several times. For generations our family had lived on the waterfront working as fishermen and sailors. My parents had been married only three years. I was just a few months old when my father was asked to deliver a shipment of dried fish to Crete. As a new father, he wasn't anxious to leave his son and wife. So he loaded us up and we headed into the open sea. That very night, one of the worst storms anyone could remember bore down on our little boat. The winds whipped the boat in circles and ripped the sail in two. Several days later, a monk from the monastery came across our boat as he was fishing. I was down in the bottom, wrapped in cloth and barely alive."

"And what about your mother and father?" asked Julio.

"My parents were never found."

Julio's eyes were wide and his jaw was dropped open. He'd never heard about his great-grandparents before. The mysteries surrounding Antonio were beginning to unravel, and he found himself hanging on every word.

"What happened next, Grandfather?"

"Not long after the accident Felipo adopted me, and I soon became the youngest member of the order," Antonio said proudly.

"Was it boring growing up in the monastery?" Julio asked innocently.

The sun was beginning to burn through the thin layer of clouds above St. Peter's, and Antonio wiped away a drop of sweat creeping near the edge of his eye. He shifted on the steps and then remembered the gardens near the plaza.

"Come, walk with me," he said as he stood and moved down the steps toward the roses that he knew were just beyond the east colonnades. "Growing up in the monastery was anything but boring. In fact, it was a lot of fun and a lot of work."

"Work?" Julio replied as he kicked a small stone from his sandal and brushed his hand across the large marble pillars near the entrance to the gardens.

"Yes, work. As soon as I learned how to walk, I was assigned simple tasks around the monastery. At first, I would do things like deliver water to the men who were working at the tables, copying the Scriptures. Then I found myself in the vineyards, picking grapes and helping with the harvest."

"How could you stand it?"

"Stand it? It didn't take long for me to discover that I loved to work . . . and think. Before long, I was working hand in hand with Felipo, developing ideas to increase the influence of the monastery. By the time I was sixteen, I had pioneered several new ways for the monks to produce their products at a bigger profit." Now Antonio was nearly skipping. Just talking about his innovations had clearly energized him.

"It didn't take long for Felipo to realize that I was passionate about business and God at the same time. It was the custom of the order that young men on their eighteenth birthday would make their decision to pursue a life of consecration as a monk, or to enter the marketplace and become a merchant. It was time for me to choose my vocation."

"Vocation? What does that mean?" asked Julio.

"It's what you do," returned Antonio.

"You mean your job?"

"Oh, it's much more than a job. You see, Julio, your vocation is your calling. It's the thing that you were born to do. And when you do it, it's not really *work* at all."

"I get it," Julio said. "You mean like father . . . and the boats. He's always on the docks with his ships, even when he doesn't have to be."

"Exactly. When a person discovers his vocation, he does it gladly and with joy."

"So what happened next, Grandfather?"

"Well, Felipo knew that it was time for me to choose my vocation, but it wasn't entirely clear if I'd be better suited in the ministry or in the marketplace. Felipo had made a special point to sit with me at the evening meal. During supper Felipo had asked me about my intentions regarding the order. I remember that without even a second thought, I had responded that I wanted to become a monk like him. Though something inside Felipo must have leapt with joy at the thought of me joining the order, he knew that I could only make the decision after fully understanding both worlds."

"Both worlds?" questioned Julio.

"The ministry and the marketplace."

"So what happened?"

"Felipo arranged for me to spend several months with a wealthy friend in Venice who lived about an hour's trek from the monastery.

"He figured this would give me an opportunity to experience the business world. That weekend we packed up and traveled into Venice, and I began my apprenticeship with Alessio."

"Alessio? That was the merchant's name?" asked Julio.

"That's right. Alessio was a wealthy merchant and a close friend of Felipo. I went to work for Alessio for several months. He was a big man with a big heart and a big business. I can still remember the first time I saw him. He must have weighed two hundred and forty pounds. He was completely bald, except for a trimmed beard that went down to his chest. He seemed to laugh every few minutes. And when he laughed, he'd make you want to laugh right along with him. He was the owner of a fleet of boats. And I was assigned to assist in managing his vessels.

"Venice had experienced booming growth after the cure for the black plague was discovered. The shipping industry was growing and was the driving force in the economy. Other merchants, including leatherworkers, blacksmiths, and stone masons, were prospering because of the influx of people streaming into the Lion City, as Venice was known. Also, the city had become famous for the glass it produced. It had experienced so much growth in that industry that the ruler, the Doge, had ordered all the kilns and glassmakers to move to Murano, an island off the coast of Venice."

"Isn't that where you live?" Julio asked.

"Yes."

"Why did the Doge move all the glassmakers?"

"Initially it was done to protect Venice from the danger of fires that were occasionally caused by the factories. But later the glassmakers were also assigned to the island to guard the secrets of their trade. Needless to say, the shipping industry worked hard to keep up with the growing economy, and Alessio's business was at the heart of it. From the time I started with Alessio, I never experienced an idle day."

"Let me guess." Julio smiled. "You loved it."

"You're catching on. After a few months of managing people, counting products, and creating new ideas, I realized that I had discovered my vocation. In fact, at the end of the two months, I was disappointed that it was over. Before I returned to the monastery, Alessio insisted that we have a supper of chicken stew together to discuss my future.

"That night my bags were packed neatly near the fireplace. Alessio had arranged for a carriage to take me back to the monastery. But I was trying to figure out how to tell Alessio that I wanted to stay with him awhile longer."

Antonio and Julio had found a small patch of grass near a towering rose bush. They had lost themselves in Antonio's story when a frail old woman waved for their attention, asking for money. Julio watched as Antonio stood and walked slowly over to the woman. He reached into his pocket and pressed a coin into the woman's hand. With a smile, the woman was gone.

"Are you hungry, Julio?" Antonio asked.

"No, not yet. I want to hear the rest of the story. What did you tell Alessio?"

"Well, I knew the decision I had to make would change my life forever, and I wanted to be sure that it was the right one. As I sat there staring at the fire, I could feel the sweat beading on my forehead. It wasn't from the heat of the flames, but from the pressure of the decision that lay just moments ahead."

"You were choosing your vocation, right?" blurted out Julio, almost running over Antonio's words.

"Exactly. It would be a decision that would change my life forever, and I wanted it to be the right one.

"I remember looking into the fire, listening to the sounds

of the crackling wood. Then I remember hearing the laugh. There was no mistaking Alessio's laugh. He burst into the room and nearly slammed every pound of his weight against me. He wrapped his short arms around me and embraced me as he always did."

"Did you tell him? Did you tell him that you wanted to be a merchant?"

"Well, yes. But not right away, and not in those words exactly. As we sat down and began our meal, I remember asking him how he first met Felipo, my father. I remember he pushed his chair away from the table and sighed deeply. 'I first met your father when I was nine years old,' he told me."

CHAPTER THREE

A TALE OF TWO MEN

J ulio suddenly realized that his stomach was churning. "I think I'm ready for lunch," he said, smiling at his grandfather.

"Let's walk down this street," suggested Antonio. "I know a man there who can help us get something to eat." The two men, nearly two generations apart, meandered down the crowded thoroughfare in the shadows of the great basilica. Julio somehow knew that this meeting and the story that was gradually unraveling would impact him deeply.

As they made their way, Julio noticed for the first time that his grandfather had a slight limp. For a moment, he wondered if something had happened to him on the way to St. Peter's. But he couldn't recall anything out of the ordinary.

Antonio interrupted his thoughts. "They were altar boys."

"You mean the monk and the merchant? They were altar boys for the church?"

"Exactly. That's how they first met. Alessio told me that he and Felipo grew up in Venice together." Smiling through his white beard, Antonio continued. "As boys, they did everything together. They went to the same school. They served in the same church. They were best friends."

"What happened to the monk and the merchant next, Grandfather?"

"Well, they weren't the monk and the merchant yet. They were still simply Felipo and Alessio. But that would all soon change. You see, as they grew older they knew that they would soon have to—"

"Choose their vocation?" piped in Julio.

"That's right. Alessio was a natural merchant. He'd worked with his father on the docks and had quickly moved through the ranks. Before long he was supervising twelve men in the boathouse. He was a natural. When it came time to announce his vocation, needless to say he had decided to join his father as a merchant."

"What happened to Felipo?" wondered Julio.

"Well, my father, as I have always called him, had known from a young age that he wanted to serve God in a monastery. In fact, Alessio told me that as a boy, Felipo was walking through some gardens one day, and he was sure that he could hear the voice of God calling to him. I remember Felipo telling me that same story many times as I grew up. Alessio said that from that day on, my father had decided to give his life to God as a monk. He was at the church whenever the doors were open. He often sat with the priests, prodding them with questions, asking them to read the Scriptures to him. And as soon as he was able, he committed himself to the order and moved to the monastery. He found me in the boat a short time later."

The smells of Roman cooking were now all around them. As Antonio and Julio walked down the stone pathway, a man with a cart stacked with fruit was working hard to sell a tomato to a young priest. The shadows of St. Peter's were behind them. But the domes and pillars and porticos still towered above everything else and served as a constant reminder that God was the first order of business here. Something about

St. Peter's brought a sense of safety and calm. Even the fruit vendor seemed to work in a hushed tone as he hawked his goods.

It was now midday, and Antonio suddenly stopped in the middle of the now-bustling street.

Although he didn't understand why, Julio followed suit and stood near his grandfather. Then it began. At first it was simply a few soft dings in the distance. Then it grew in intensity and rhythm. Julio couldn't keep the smile from his face.

"The bells. Are they coming from the basilica?" he asked.

"Yes. Every day, twice a day, the bells ring as worship to God. Every year a few more bells are added," Antonio said, pausing every few words to take in the sounds.

Julio was sure he recognized a hymn he'd heard somewhere before. It didn't matter. This was one of the greatest moments of his life. He would remember it forever. The cathedral towering above them. The streets filled with wonder and worship. The people working hard and honoring God at the same time. And his grandfather standing by his side. His thoughts were suddenly interrupted, and he noticed that his grandfather had started walking again and had moved several steps ahead of him. He rushed to catch up and then settled into pace.

"Were they still friends after your father moved to the monastery?"

"Of course they were. At least at first. You see, Alessio quickly became even more successful than his father had been, and his business grew to become one of the largest trading empires in the region. Meanwhile, my father, who was also a natural leader, was selected to be the abbot, the head monk of the monastery.

"As the abbot, Felipo also had the responsibility of coordinating mass at the cathedral in Venice. For the first few years, Alessio would go to the church twice a week to see his friend and worship God. But as his business grew, his visits slowed to once a week."

"Did your father care?"

"Yes. You see, my father was so passionate about God, he couldn't imagine why anyone wouldn't want to spend every day in the church. For him, it was where he felt most alive. And that's what happens when you discover your true vocation. Anyway, my father, Felipo, began to resent the fact that Alessio was at church only once a week. Alessio told me that Felipo began to make comments about serving God and the importance of mass, in hopes that out of guilt Alessio might be more frequent in his visits to the church. Alessio began to feel as though Felipo was pressuring him, and for a while the two men drifted apart."

As they walked, Julio wondered if that would happen to him and his friend Ricardo. He couldn't imagine anything coming between them. And he suddenly felt badly for the two best friends who had drifted apart. "What happened next?"

"Well, nothing happened for a long time. The two men were committed to their vocations, and both excelled. A new church was built to accommodate the additional people that loved God and wanted to hear Felipo teach from the Scriptures. At the same time, Alessio's shipping empire had become the largest in the Mediterranean. There were over one hundred boats with his family's name sailing the sea, delivering goods. Alessio continued to attend weekly mass, and Felipo continued to secretly wish that Alessio was there more often. But they spoke to each other less and less . . . until one day."

Just then a large man, at least two barrels wide, nearly slammed into Julio, who barely stepped out of the way in time. The man reached out his arms and wrapped them around Antonio's waist, lifting him into the air. Julio watched half in horror and half in disbelief as the short man spun his grandfather around twice and then dropped him to the ground. For a moment, Julio wondered if he should do anything to help. But then the laughter gave it away. He watched as the two men embraced and chortled in the middle of the street. Julio felt a twinge of embarrassment, as he realized that the rest of the street vendors and people had quieted and were watching them.

"Venito, this is my grandson, Julio," Antonio said proudly. "Julio, Venito has been part of our family now for nearly thirty-five years. We first met on a fishing expedition off the coast of Murano. Even then, he was the finest cook on the island. We quickly became friends, and his family frequently welcomed me into their home. He eventually opened a café of his own."

"Yes, yes, Julio. What Antonio hasn't told you is that he taught me the secrets of becoming a wise businessman. In fact, I owe much of who I am now to Antonio." Venito gave Antonio an appreciative glance.

Julio extended his hand toward Venito, poising himself for a potential arm-wrap and swing. To Julio's relief, Venito graciously returned the handshake and pointed toward a small canopy with three tables tucked neatly under it.

"Come and enjoy lunch in my new restaurant. I opened this café just a month ago. That makes nine," he said proudly.

The three men walked over to a table and settled into their chairs, as Venito shouted orders to another round man who was carving a juicy roasted lamb. Julio could feel his mouth begin to water. In what seemed like seconds, a large portion was placed in front of Julio and Antonio. After a short prayer, Venito excused himself.

"Please enjoy your meal. I must go now to attend to my other cafés. It has been good to see you both." With that, Venito stood and began to walk down the street, quickly joined by several other men. Antonio continued his story.

"One day while Felipo was reading the Scriptures, he found something, something special."

"What did he find?" Julio asked anxiously.

"He found a verse that explained what had happened to him and Alessio. He quickly sent an altar boy to find Alessio and ask him to come to the cathedral. Within an hour, Alessio was there. Felipo took Alessio to a room behind the altar where a copy of the sacred writings was kept. The copy of the Scripture at the church was one of only several hundred complete manuscripts in the world. Alessio understood the significance of the room with its treasure and was honored to be there. As the two men walked in, Felipo pointed to the large volume that was opened to a page near the end."

"What did he find there? What verse did Felipo find that was so meaningful?" Julio had stopped eating his lamb and was now engrossed in the story again.

"The verse says that God 'has made us kings and priests . . .'"

"I don't understand," retorted Julio. "Alessio wasn't a king. What was he trying to say?"

"Julio, that day God revealed to Felipo that Alessio was indeed a king. Not a king as we think of kings, though. You see, the verse says that God continues to make us kings and priests. That means that He's still doing it. God was saying that He calls some of us to be priests and some of us to be merchants, or kings."

"Oh, I get it. A king is like a man who runs a business, right?"

"That's right. That day God revealed to my father that he was a priest, called to hear from God and to lead others into God's presence. But God also revealed that Alessio was a king, called to take dominion in the marketplace and provide resources to fulfill the vision of the priests. That day Felipo repented to Alessio for judging him and placing unrealistic expectations on him. He knew that he had been trying to make him into a priest when Alessio was really a king. He understood that it was his role to bless Alessio with encouragement from God and His Word. At that point the two men were reunited as friends, and each was more effective as they realized how they could work together in partnership."

"So priests are supposed to serve God, and businessmen are supposed to serve the priests, right?"

"No, that's not what I mean. You see, God has made all of us to serve Him. We are all called to hear from God and honor His Word. We are all called to live our lives in a way that glorifies Him. But God has created a special relationship between people in the marketplace and those who have committed their lives to serve God as their vocation."

"I think I understand. God gives businessmen the resources to help fulfill the calling of the priests, who have given their own time and resources specifically to serving God and to blessing the businessmen."

"That's right. It's a very special sort of partnership," explained Antonio.

"Is that the end of the story?" Julio wondered.

"No, it's not nearly the end. It's really just the beginning. After Alessio told me the story of how he had met my father, and how they had discovered together the importance of teaming up as kings and priests, he asked me what I had decided about my vocation."

"I know this part. You became a merchant, I mean a king, right?"

"That's right. That night, as we ate chicken stew and talked about kings and priests, I told Alessio that I wanted to become a merchant. I knew that my calling was to produce goods and services and to provide resources to empower the priests to fulfill their vision for the kingdom of God. And I was ready. Well, sort of, anyway."

"What do you mean, 'sort of'?"

"I was ready to begin my work as a merchant. But I knew that I still had a lot to learn. I had only worked for Alessio for two months. I still had so many questions. That night I asked him if he would be willing to mentor me as I developed as a king."

"What did he say?"

"He accepted, with one condition."

"One condition?"

"Yes. He told me that he'd mentor me in business if I would commit to meet him at his house on this same evening once every three years. He told me that he wanted to help me as I developed and that he wanted to hold me accountable for what I learned."

"What did you say?"

"I accepted, of course. He also instructed me to keep a journal of all that I learned from him. And I did. I recorded the events and words of every visit." With that, Antonio reached down and pushed his hand into a leather satchel that had been swinging at his side. He pulled out an old book, covered in leather and obviously well-worn. It was a square binding with faded gold lettering on the front. It faintly read *The Journal of a King.* The edges of the pages were frayed, but they appeared to be still intact. There was a gold clasp that attached the front of the book to the back.

"In this are written the lessons that I learned over the years that I met with Alessio. The words in this book have helped me to create for myself a life beyond my wildest dreams. The ideas that Alessio taught me, the ideas in this book, are the principles that I have applied to my business and to my life. They have helped to expand my opportunities and multiply my wealth."

Julio was suddenly aware of the gravity of his visit to Rome. He understood that his grandfather had taken him on this journey to reveal to him the secrets to his great fortune, and he wasn't about to pass up this opportunity to learn. He hesitated for a moment, unsure of how to respond. And then he boldly asked, "Grandfather, would you share the words in your journal with me?"

"Yes, my son, I will."

Antonio slowly opened the front cover. A million pictures and memories flashed into Antonio's mind as he remembered his first visit with Alessio. Three years had passed. And as he had promised, he prepared to meet with his friend.

CHAPTER FOUR

THE FIRST MEETING

The glow coming from the lantern hanging in front of Alessio's house danced out across the water and formed a fan of light on the face of the canal. It was just enough for me to see the outline of the docks. For a moment I wondered if this was a good idea. But a deal was a deal. As I neared the dock, a familiar sight came into focus. Ten cargo ships, with their sails neatly tucked under the massive riggings, were a dead giveaway. I knew that Alessio was the only merchant who organized his armada that way. After all, I had been the one to instigate that new organization of boats during my summer with the merchant.

I was alone. It had been part of the deal. Every three years. He had carefully instructed me to meet him right here at this house, every three years, on this day and at this hour . . . alone. I had wondered why Alessio had chosen such an odd time to meet together. But that was his personality. He was always trying to leave me guessing.

I didn't see him at first. As my small boat approached the dock, I lifted my foot over the side of the hull and jumped onto the wooden planks. The old boards creaked under my feet as I spun around to grab the rope and secure it to a nearby post. My movements on the dock were quick and precise. I recalled the hundreds of times I had tied and untied these boats.

I was eager to tell Alessio about the adventures of my first three years in business. I also needed to get his advice on a few things that had been troubling me. I grabbed my small pack from my boat and headed for the large, stone house. As

I moved away from the water, I caught sight of something out of the corner of my eye. A light?

I spun around to see a small lantern flickering near the edge of the water, about twenty yards away. The light from the lantern must have blended in with the light coming from the house. My instinct told me to stay on course and keep walking. But my curiosity won over. I turned sharply and began to make my way slowly toward the dim light. As I walked past a row of boats, I wondered what had become of Alessio during the last three years. I tensed as I neared the light. I could make out the faint outline of a man sitting on a crude stool. A sudden laugh broke the silence.

Alessio stood with the candle to his face. A broad smile revealed his teeth. I dropped my pack and began to walk quickly toward him. I think it was something about his smile that made me feel as though everything would be okay.

"My friend, it is good to see you," Alessio said warmly.

I returned the greeting. "It's good to see you too." Strolling back to the house, the two of us laughed and talked. As we approached, I couldn't help but be reminded of the days I had served side by side with Alessio's dockhands, unloading silk from the Orient and reloading marble and glass on its way to France.

I remembered how sometimes in one week, we'd see more than a hundred boats unload their goods in this harbor. I had never really realized how influential and wealthy Alessio had become. But one day I had added up one month's profits from the ships, and it was more than most businessmen would make during an entire lifetime. I was amazed at the simple way this successful merchant lived and yet maintained one of the greatest business empires in the world. And I was determined to learn from him.

As we walked into the house, I was greeted by the aroma of something wonderful brewing in the kitchen around the corner. The fire was already warming the room, and I instantly felt like I was home. After greeting the staff, we both sat down at a dark brown wooden table. Its large legs had ornate carvings. I had never seen anything like it. I figured it had been one of Alessio's special imports, probably from across the sea.

"From Asia?" I asked. The design of the carvings and the type of wood was typical of the kind imported from the Far East.

"Yes, China to be precise. Made by some of their finest craftsmen over a century ago. I bought it in exchange for linen and wine. What do you think?"

"I think it's fantastic! That you're trading with the East, I mean. Oh, and yes, the table is magnificent." I ran my fingers across an exquisite carving of a lion that was at least two feet from nose to tail and had its mouth open in an imposing roar. The lion was certainly appropriate for Venice. It was the symbol of St. Mark, the patron saint of the city. The table measured almost six feet long and was the focal point of the room.

"The gates to the world have opened to us here in Venice, Antonio. It seems as though we've become a crossroads to the world of trade. Thousands of boats and caravans come in and out of Venice every year. I only wish we had a better system of exchange. It's difficult to be competitive when the other merchants are offering less than I am in return for the same goods."

"That's not fair to you," I said, almost wanting to egg him on. During my years away from Alessio, I had discovered what I thought could be a new method of trade, and I was hoping to have the opportunity to ask him about it. I thought this might be my chance.

"Well, it's not exactly their fault. There is just no way to be fair when so many different goods are used in trade. I mean, who can determine the value of a camel versus grain versus glass? It's all so subjective—" Alessio began.

Before he could say anything else, I interrupted him. "What if . . . what if you could trade with a universally accepted currency?" I asked, eager to tell Alessio about my new idea.

"Well, that would be a miracle. But how? I mean, with the world's economy growing every day, it's become nearly impossible to purchase any goods with money, even with the currency of a nearby city!"

I was wearing a burgundy-colored cloak made of wool with leather trim around the edges. Smiling, I reached into a small pocket on the inside chest of the cloak and withdrew a small leather pouch. As I did, the contents of the pouch created a slight clinking, like the sound of broken shells against stone. I handed the pouch to Alessio.

"Open it," I challenged him.

He untied the pouch and carefully emptied its contents into his palm. In his hand were ten meticulously crafted glass beads. Designed as cylinders, the beads were a unique combination of blues and reds and whites swirled together. Each was no more than an inch in diameter and had a hole through the center.

"Glass beads?" he said, quite surprised and a bit amused. Although he knew the skill of the Murano glassmakers, he had never seen beads made in the fashion as the ones in his hand.

"Oh, not just any beads. About two months ago, I was on a trade journey to Sicily, and I stopped on the island of Murano. While I was there, a gentleman told me about a family who had invented a new method of making glass beads. The results were beads that could not be duplicated by anyone else."

"Go on," Alessio said, suddenly engrossed in this new story.

"Well, I was blindfolded and taken on horseback to the house of a merchant family. When I arrived, I told the glassmaker that I had heard about his method of making glass beads that were impossible to duplicate. He nodded, and I was presented with a handful of beads, the ones in your hand now. I remember telling the man that I doubted whether his claims were true. The merchant challenged me to have the finest glassmakers on Murano try to copy the beads. He told me that if I could do it, he'd give me his entire glass factory."

"Well?" said Alessio.

"I tried. It was impossible. Five different glassmakers, the finest in the region, all failed. As soon as I discovered that the beads were unique, I realized that they could be used as a universal currency. Finally, the trade-world would have access to a currency that could be used by all merchants . . . if I could only convince businesses to use my beads, that is."

"So what did you do next?" asked Alessio.

"I returned to the merchant and bought the rights to be the sole distributor of his beads. Alessio, I think I've discovered the solution to your trade problems. I think I've discovered a universal currency."

After a short pause, Alessio's response was immediate and calculated. He stood from the table and said, "I'll use them. In fact, I'll take as many as you can produce, and I'll begin to distribute them as my new method of payment. Please, if you'll allow me to keep these beads, I will have a messenger send them to my largest customers and notify them of the news. If you are sure you want to proceed, that is."

I didn't know how to respond. "Of course I want to proceed. Alessio, I don't know what to say. I . . ."

∽

Julio couldn't help himself any longer. He had been sitting there, absorbing the story, ignoring his lunch. He suddenly blurted out, "The beads . . . were they Venitian trade beads?"

"Yes, the first ones. I eventually bought the bead factory and began distributing my beads around the world," replied Antonio.

"But the trade beads are everywhere now. I mean, they're used all over the world. That was your idea?" Julio knew that his grandfather was an influential businessman, but he had no idea exactly how influential. As he was growing up, Julio would visit his grandfather on Murano. And he had even worked on his docks last summer. But the source of his wealth had always been a mystery. Until now. Venetian trade beads had become the standard currency for nearly all the trade in Europe and Asia. His mind whirred as he attempted to calculate the value of the beads and accumulated wealth they would have produced for Antonio. His thoughts finally slowed. Julio shook his head in disbelief and repeated his question again.

"You mean, you created the idea of using trade beads for import and export?"

"Yes, Julio, that was me. It was an idea that I believe God Himself gave to me." For a moment the two of them sat in silence as the young man absorbed the weight of his new discovery.

Antonio turned the page of the book in his hands and laid it down on the table in front of him. With his eyes still connected with Julio's, he spun the book around so it faced his grandson.

"This is the first secret to success," he said as he pointed to the only writing on that page. Julio looked down at the book and read the words out loud.

PRINCIPLE ONE:
WORK HARD AND GOD WILL PROSPER YOU.

"What does it mean, Grandfather?" Julio asked.

"It means that hard work is the beginning of success. Scripture tells us that God will bless 'all the work of your hand,' if you are faithful to Him. You see, a lot of people have a great idea—"

"Like the Venetian trade beads?"

"Yes, like the trade beads. They have a great idea, but they never do anything about it. The first principle that Alessio taught me was the importance of working hard at something you believe in. It's easy to have an idea. But it's another thing to commit time and effort to it."

"Grandfather, I have a good friend whose father says he has a new way to irrigate the fields. But his father says that the other farmers are keeping him from doing anything with his idea."

"Julio, there are a lot of great ideas. But if we allow the negative influences of others to stop us, then we will never accomplish anything. The truth is, most people are always waiting to begin, but few ever actually get on the pathway to success."

"Yes, but if God wants you to succeed, won't He bless you regardless of what you do?"

"That is one of the great misunderstandings that we often have of God. You see, God *does* want to bless us. But He will only bless what we actually put our hands to. God wants us to seek His guidance and then work hard. In fact, Paul once said that if a man doesn't work, he shouldn't eat. Those are pretty strong words. But God wants us to understand the importance of diligence."

Julio was recording every word in his mind. He knew that these principles of success had worked for Alessio and Felipo and Antonio. Surely they could work for him too. He was anxious to hear the rest of the ideas in the book, but he wanted to be sure that he understood the first principle before they moved on.

"So the first principle is basically, 'Seek God and decide what you want to do, and then do whatever it takes to make it happen.' Oh, and work hard at it. If I do this, getting help when I need it, God will bless whatever I do. Is that it?"

Antonio smiled. He knew that a valuable treasure was being passed to a new generation. "Yes, work hard, Julio, at something you love, and eventually you will see the blessing of God in what you do."

"Was that the end of your first meeting with Alessio, Grandfather?" asked Julio.

"Yes, that was it. I left his house late that evening and sailed back to my own home. Later the next day, I went to a friend who was a leather merchant, and I had him bind this book. In it I wrote all the ideas that I had learned during my first visit with Alessio. For three years, I worked hard at developing the idea of the Venetian trade beads. He was right. Hard work paid off. And then I eagerly awaited my second visit with him."

CHAPTER FIVE

THE SECOND MEETING

This time I'd be ready. Three years before, Alessio had nearly scared me to death on the dock with his candle, so my approach had to be virtually undetectable. I was thankful for the slight cloud cover that evening, and I was grateful for the new boat. It seemed to move through the water without as much as a single sound. The slanted bow and deeper hull made the journey easy. Three years before, I wouldn't have dreamed that I would be in this new boat. The boat I had docked at Alessio's house for our first meeting was more than twenty years old. I had grown accustomed to carrying a small jar with me in order to bail the water out of the bottom. This vessel was very different.

I had bought the boat about a month before from an artisan on Murano. He was one of the finest boat makers on the sea. I had dealt with him many times when I was working on the docks for Alessio. I remember how surprised the boat maker was to see me, and how more surprised he was when I told him about the boat that I wanted to buy. He had said that he would only accept trade beads as payment for the boat.

"This is the only way I can guarantee that you actually have the money," he had explained.

I smiled as I handed him a bag of beads that he carefully counted and recounted until he was satisfied. I recall the feeling of realizing that my beads were being used across the region. The words from three years before echoed in my mind as I paddled the final kilometer toward Alessio's house.

WORK HARD AND GOD WILL PROSPER YOU.

They had been simple words, and yet so powerful. After the first meeting at Alessio's house, I began to strategize how I could expand the influence and opportunities of the beads. It was hard work. But within six months several key merchants were using the beads for their trading. Within three years, the beads had become the standard in Venice. For the first time in my life, I was beginning to accumulate money. The past years had not been easy, though. My friends and even my family wondered about my new success. I was eager to meet with Alessio and get his counsel about the future. There were so many new questions and new challenges.

I had to focus to make out the lines of the shore. I searched to find the familiar boat dock. For a moment, I wondered if it had disappeared or if Alessio had moved his operations altogether. He had talked once about moving his company to the northern edge of the city where the majority of the trading was transacted. *Surely he would have contacted me if he had moved,* I thought.

Then I saw it.

The same old dock with the same boats carefully tied to the wooden posts. The dock was deserted. I quickly scanned it in search of a low flame or a crouching man, but I saw nothing.

I then eased my way in and jumped out onto the planks. I tied my new boat to the post and quickly walked up and down the pier expecting to find my friend. This time he wasn't waiting, at least not here. I walked toward the house. As I approached the front door, I noticed that there were no lights. There was no smell of fine cooking floating through the air. As I drew closer to the entry, I saw a small paper folded in half and stuck onto the door with a short nail. It was addressed to me.

I quickly pulled the sheet from the door and opened it. There was a short message with instructions written in black ink. It read:

> *Meet me at the church near the mill. Mass begins at midnight.*
> *Do not be late. Welcome, my friend.*
>
> *—Alessio*

I reread the note and then wondered why he had arranged to meet me at the church. I checked to see if I had all of my belongings. I estimated that it would take me thirty minutes to walk. Even though there was a carriage readily available at the stables a few yards down the street, I decided it would be welcome exercise to go by foot.

As I set out, I reached down into the leather pouch hanging over my shoulder. My fingers felt the edges of the journal that I had purchased three years before. Since my last meeting with Alessio, I had kept a sort of diary of my business and personal affairs. I was eager to share it with Alessio and add other principles to it.

The clouds broke up over my head. The moon shone down

on the path in front of me, illuminating the dirt at my feet and the rooftops of the houses scattered along the road. The smells and sounds of the nearby canal suddenly reminded me of the long nights that I had spent with Felipo talking about God. We would sit on the edge of the canal and look up at the stars, and he'd tell me about the greatness of our Creator.

Something about those evenings had forever reassured me. In fact, every time I looked up at the heavens at night, I remembered the words: "For I know the thoughts that I think toward you, says the LORD, thoughts of peace and not of evil, to give you a future and a hope."

As I shuffled along the road that night, I whispered several prayers to God: prayers of gratitude for the life He'd blessed me with, but also prayers of guidance. Guidance for the tough decisions that I was struggling with in my heart.

I could hear the sounds of people gathering somewhere from the road ahead, and I realized that it must be the church preparing for midnight mass. It wasn't normal for a church to have mass at midnight during the summer months. But it had become a sort of tradition at this particular church. I remember during the months that I worked on the docks, Alessio left the house late on Saturday evenings to seek after God.

The church was very simple but elegant. It must have been fifty feet long and thirty feet wide, with a large archway over the front door. It had several stained-glass windows, each at least fifteen feet high stretching from the ceiling to the ground. On one of the windows there was a beautiful picture of St. Thomas, and on another a picture of Moses carrying the Ten Commandments. *The principles of God*, I thought to myself as I walked closer to the church.

The doors were open and several people were gathering inside. I quickly scanned the sanctuary for Alessio but with no luck. I then eased my way into a pew in the back of the church. As I did, two altar boys dressed in white passed by me. I smiled as I remembered the stories that Alessio had told me about him and Felipo. Suddenly, I heard a sound and I spun around. I saw Alessio sitting in the corner by himself. I wasn't sure how I had missed him. He smiled his usual broad grin and waved for me to join him.

We greeted one another and then quietly waited for the service to begin.

As I sat in the church that evening, I couldn't help but remember the days and nights spent at the monastery. How different my life had now become! At the monastery I had learned to go for long periods of time without talking. Now I was known for my ability to communicate with others. At the monastery I had little or no contact with women, because we had all made a vow of celibacy. Now I was considering the idea of marriage for the first time. At the monastery I owned nothing. Now I had boats and employees, and I was building my wealth.

My thoughts were suddenly interrupted by the familiar sounds of the liturgy I loved and knew so well. I stood and spoke the holy words along with the several dozen others at the mass that evening. The priest stood to read from the Scriptures before communion. For the next few moments, he read the familiar words of Jesus regarding the rich young ruler. He noted that the man was told to sell everything he had and to give it to the poor.

As the priest said these words, I couldn't help but notice that it seemed as though he was looking directly at Alessio, who had a pleasant smile on his face during the entire sermon. The priest then told us that Jesus had said that it would be more difficult for a rich man to enter into heaven than for a camel to go through the eye of a needle. Again, I could sense an unspoken exchange between the priest and my friend. I couldn't help but feel guilty about my own wealth. After all, I had left a life that was totally submitted to God to . . . pursue profit? I shook my head and tried to concentrate on the rest of the sermon.

After a few more words, the priest prepared for Holy Communion, and we walked together down the center aisle to receive the elements and worship God. As we left the church that evening, the words of the sermon echoed in my head until they were interrupted by the voice of my friend.

"How are you, Antonio?" Alessio asked. "I have heard a good deal about your glass. I see that you have learned well." Alessio spoke with the tone of a proud father. I didn't mind. After all, he was my mentor and teacher.

"Yes, Alessio, it has been a good time for me. After our meeting, I began to apply the first principle, and I've had fantastic results. My business has grown, and I now have more wealth than I ever thought I'd have. Of course, I've also had new challenges." I said this with a slight frown, as I recalled all the people who seemed to resent me. I suddenly thought of the priest.

"Alessio."

"Yes, my friend. What is troubling you?"

"The priest. I wish it didn't bother me so much. But I just can't seem to get over his words about rich men and the kingdom of God." I said it almost half-afraid of discussing a forbidden subject.

With a smile on his face Alessio said, "Antonio, I understand how you feel. I knew the priest would read that verse tonight. He is actually my good friend. We often spend time together. He means well. He simply misunderstands the meaning of the verses."

"But—"

"Yes, I know. He is very passionate about the rich giving to the poor. Antonio, Jesus always deals with us one-on-one. That means that He sees every one of our lives as independent . . . as special. You see, when Jesus was talking to the rich young ruler, He was dealing with *him* specifically, not *everyone* generally. Jesus knew that the young man had made an idol out of money, and He wanted the man to be free. He knew that the only way for the man to be free was to get rid of the thing that held him captive."

"Money?"

"Precisely."

"How do you know that Jesus wasn't talking to everyone?"

"Well, for one thing, a few verses later the disciples asked Jesus the same question. They said, 'Lord, if this man isn't going to enter the kingdom of heaven, then how can we?' They were saying this because many of them knew what it was like to come from great wealth."

"Really?"

"Yes. In fact, James and John were the sons of Zebedee, a successful fishing merchant. And Peter was a partner in their fishing business." Alessio smiled as he recalled the scriptural fact to me.

"Besides, Jesus encountered other men of considerable wealth and never asked them to sell all their things. Zebedee, Zaccheus, Matthew the tax collector, the Roman officer, and Nicodemus, just to name a few. It seems that Jesus was more interested in dealing with each of them individually, based on their specific situations, based on their heart and their motives. And remember, Jesus also said in that same chapter regarding entrance into heaven that through man it is impossible, but that through God all things are possible."

"Yes. But what about the part with the camel?"

Alessio was walking quickly now. I could make out his house a few yards ahead in the road. I could clearly see a light coming from somewhere in the house, and I was secretly hoping that someone was hard at work in the kitchen.

"Antonio, I have been to Jerusalem several times. I've been

told that in ancient days the walled cities were often protected by cutting small doors into the city gates so that man and beast could only enter the city by literally getting on their knees. Those small doors were commonly called the 'eye of the needle.'"

"So it *was* possible for a camel to get through the eye of the needle," I returned. "It just meant that for it to happen, the camel had to get down on its knees . . . just like men of wealth. We've got to humble ourselves and get down on our knees to make it through life successfully . . . and please God."

"That's right."

"But tonight I heard the priest say something about the importance of giving away one's wealth. He warned against the rich living so comfortably that there would be nothing left for the poor."

We had arrived back at Alessio's house. The front door was now open a few inches, just enough to let the smell of ministrone distract me for a moment. Alessio pushed the door open and stepped inside. He waved his hand in the direction of the Chinese table still situated in the middle of the room.

"Come and sit down, Antonio. You must be hungry."

We prayed over our meal, and then spent several minutes devouring the spicy vegetable soup and warm bread with fresh butter. Alessio was the first to break the silence.

"Well, it's true that some people see wealth or resources as a single pie." He reached over and placed a round fruit pie in the center of the table. "They think that if someone gets too big of a piece, then there won't be enough left for anyone else."

As he said this, he cut a slice of the pie and placed it on his own plate. "It's just not true. You see, unlike this one pie, God's resources are infinite. And His will is to prosper us, so that we can in turn help to expand His kingdom here on earth. God can make as many pies as He pleases."

"And what about the people who say that the merchants are simply gaining profits at the expense of the people?" I asked as I cut a piece of pie for myself.

"Yes, yes. They are the same ones that fail to understand the ideas of enterprise. You see, when a merchant sells a product or a service to a customer, then as long as it is ethical, everyone wins. The customer wins because he can now use the new product to make his life better. And the merchant wins because he has made a profit on the valuable product that he has offered. Julio, this notion that wealth is evil is simply a lie."

As I finished the fruit pie in front of me, I wanted to be sure that I had asked Alessio all that I had on my mind. And there were still a few things that I was struggling with.

"Alessio, I don't mean to be argumentative. But I have so many questions."

He nodded, as if to give me permission to continue.

"I have several friends, men that I grew up with in the monastery. They love God and they love me. But they often tell me that God does not want me to be wealthy. They tell me that God wants me to be poor, like the monks who have made a vow of poverty."

"That's entirely different." Alessio pushed his plate away and folded his hands in front of his face, with his elbows on the table. I could tell that he was preparing to make a significant point. "Scripture tells us plainly, 'Beloved, I pray that you may prosper in all things and be in health, just as your soul prospers.' Now, I understand that your friends must obey what God tells them. Because they are monks, they are specifically obeying God's call. And that is honorable, and they will be blessed in other ways because of it. You must understand that God desires for your soul to prosper above all else. That means that God wants to know you intimately. He wants to be a significant part of your life. But unless He specifically calls you to a vow of poverty, as your relationship with Him grows, then He wants you to prosper financially."

"But does He want us to have everything or just the simple things we need to get by?"

"Jesus tells us to seek first the kingdom of God, and then all these things will be added to you. God says it this way, 'Delight yourself in the Lord, and He will give you the desires of your heart.' That means that if you are delighting in Him, seeking after Him and honoring Him, His desires will naturally become your desires. Yes, God wants you to have everything your heart desires as long as you are focused first on Him. Remember, though, that God measures our hearts and knows our motives. We must love Him for who He is, not for what He can give us."

My mind was spinning with all the new ideas that I'd

heard. I wanted to remember every word. I could hardly wait to leave that evening to write in my journal.

∽

Julio had been sitting, focused on Antonio and the account of his second meeting with Alessio. He suddenly looked down and remembered the leather book on the table. He glanced at his grandfather, who nodded approval, and then he reached down to turn the pages. He saw the words written by themselves in the center. He read them out loud.

PRINCIPLE TWO:
FINANCIAL PROSPERITY IS OFTEN
CONNECTED TO SOUL PROSPERITY.

Julio stored these precious words in his memory.

"I think I've got it so far, Grandfather. Was that the end of your second visit?"

Antonio had a grin on his face. "Not quite. I had one more thing that I wanted to ask Alessio."

∽

I remember a quiet pause as we finished our late-night supper and our discussion about the importance of soul prosperity. Alessio was the first to talk.

"Now, besides business, how are you, Antonio?"

"Well, there is one more thing . . ."

"Yes, what is it?"

"Well . . . there's this girl," I said, squeezing my eyes shut to keep from seeing Alessio's reaction.

I didn't have to see it. I heard it. He laughed long and loud. The Chinese table under our elbows shook violently with the rhythm of his belly. I struggled to open my eyes and slowly focused on Alessio's smile hidden behind his beard. I could take it. After all, I knew that his advice on the matter would be worth any amount of punishment. Over the years, I had watched him and his wife. I knew that they had a secret that I needed.

"A girl? What's her name?" he asked through his chuckling teeth.

"Maria. She's perfect, Alessio. I tell you she's perfect. We have so much in common, and Felipo loves her too. Oh, and she makes me laugh. Did I mention that she is the most beautiful woman in the region?"

"Well, it sounds like you don't need much of my counsel on this one. As long as you know you can provide for her needs, take the next step."

"Provide for her needs?" I asked.

"Yes. God compares a man who does not provide for his family with someone who has denied the faith. He considers him worse than an unbeliever. You must be able to take care of her before you marry her. And once you are married, you must do whatever it takes to provide for her. Those are God's principles, not mine."

I turned the page in the leather book and wrote:

PRINCIPLE THREE:
A MAN MUST DO WHATEVER HE CAN
TO PROVIDE FOR HIS FAMILY.

I assured Alessio that I could take care of her needs. I reminded him that the trading beads had made me a small fortune during the previous three years. He nodded his approval, and we talked and laughed into the early morning hours. He then walked me to my new boat, which I proudly showed him. Before I knew it, I was leaving. I remember waving good-bye to my good friend, wondering what the next three years would hold for me. I could hardly wait. Everything about the future seemed filled with promise.

I couldn't have been more wrong.

CHAPTER SIX

THe THIRD MEETING

It was a night that I will never forget. I had just finished counting the trading bead inventory with Milos, my business manager and close friend. I had first met Milos during a trading trip to Greece, where he had been working as a stonecutter for a local merchant. His family had been stonecutters in Greece for five generations, and he was the youngest of four brothers who had also chosen the family trade. As I talked with him, I discovered that although he loved his work, he longed for a new challenge. We had a lot in common: a zest for life, a penchant for fine craftsmanship, and a love for fishing. I asked Milos to join me in the bead business, and he accepted. Within weeks we had become close friends.

We enjoyed each other's company, and when we weren't planning the future of the business, we were fishing. He was only twenty-two when he moved to Murano. But at five feet eleven, he was taller than anyone else on the island. This gave him an instant, albeit unearned, credibility. He was a fast learner and hard worker, and quickly rose to the top of the company. Within several months he was working as the lead designer. With Milos at the helm of the product line, and me running the day-to-day operations, things really started to move. Our business was growing faster than we could manage, so we were planning an expansion of the already-crowded glass factory.

I can remember the sound. Milos and I were walking toward the dock, preparing to pack my boat for my scheduled trip to visit Alessio. There was a deep muffled rumbling coming from the direction of the factory. We both turned our heads toward the sound, only to see a tower of flames shooting thirty feet into the air. For a moment we stood frozen. Then we ran.

I could feel my feet working to move under my legs. But I remember feeling like I was losing control. My legs gave way about forty yards from the burning building. I tried in vain to throw my hands in front of me to stop the fall. My face hit the ground with a thud, and my bare chest scraped hard against the shells and sand. Milos stopped, spun around, and reached down to help me. Arm in arm, we ran awkwardly toward the flames.

The east side was the first part to fall. The seething flames engulfed it, and within minutes it collapsed to the ground. Several of the factory workers had gathered around to help as best they could. I instructed them to form a line from the beach to the building. And they were now passing crude buckets up toward the fire. Even though the water did little to slow down the destruction, the men kept working.

The building was fifty years old. It was no more than twelve feet high, with a roof and walls that were constructed of raw-cut lumber found on the island. It had never been an impressive building, but it had served its purpose. The original structure had been about twenty feet wide by fifty feet long. Milos and I had recently added another thirty feet to its width.

Ever since I had purchased the operation six years earlier, a guard had been assigned to watch the doors. Fortunately, he was the only one around when the building caught on fire. And now I could see him standing safely near what remained of the front entrance.

The north wall teetered dangerously near the heads of the would-be rescue workers. Someone yelled a warning. They all moved just in time, and I watched as a huge twenty-foot-long section came crashing to the ground. The fire was now licking the tops of the nearby palm trees, and I later learned that it could easily be seen from the neighboring islands.

The building was situated close to the docks, and before anyone thought to move the boats, flames had ignited the dock and had worked their way to the boats themselves. As the fire burned itself out, the early light of dawn mixed with the smoke. Milos walked toward me and handed me a small wooden box, on which he had written an inscription with charcoal that he'd found in the ashes. I could see that his face had been badly burned.

As he turned to walk away, I opened the box and found four small glass beads and a piece of parchment with diagrams written on it. I assumed that these were the treasured instructions detailing the secret process. I could feel my eyes filling with tears as I looked down at the only remains of my life, my career, and my wealth. "It's over," I said to myself, slowly closing the box.

I was alone now. I lowered my head and began to weep. I had failed. The box fell from my hands and onto the ground. As the box lay there in front of me, I saw the words that Milos had inscribed: "With this, we begin again." He seemed to have such faith. I wasn't so hopeful. I thought of Milos and his family in Greece. He relied on me now, and I had let him down.

The pain in my chest was more than I could bear. I suddenly felt sick and I thought I would vomit. My legs were like lead beneath me again, and I sat down on a rock nearby. "Why, God?" I asked, feeling completely alone and afraid. "Why?"

At that moment, I felt a hand on my shoulder. I brushed my face in a vain attempt to hide my emotions and glanced up to see the face. I already knew who it was. Maria. She was still as beautiful as the day I had met her. Her long dark hair and white skin had made her stand out from the plain girls of the village. She was different. Maria had worked two summers on her father's fishing boat side by side with the men. She understood the importance of hard work, and it was a good thing too. Being three months pregnant, she was about to discover the hard work that family life could be.

But now everything seemed different. Our security, our hopes, our dreams. They all were gone. As soon as I saw Maria, I was unable to contain the flood behind my eyes, and I burst into uncontrollable tears. I slumped off the stone that I had been sitting on and clutched her ankles. As I lay there in a heap on the ground, she stooped to be with me. I could feel her hand brushing the sweat and tears and soot from my face, and I could hear her voice whispering in my ear. "Don't be afraid. I love you. I'll always love you. We'll begin again.

We can always begin again." She said the words so gently and so warmly that I actually believed them, at least for a moment. After what seemed like an eternity, I lifted myself off the ground and embraced her.

"Antonio, if God is for us, who can be against us?"

I began to say something, but she stopped me by putting her finger to my lips. "Shhh," she said. "Let's walk back to the house together. There's someone there who wants to see you."

The two of us began to make our way back toward the village. As we walked, the morning sun was just peeking out over the horizon onto the water. The light cast a hundred lines of color on the glistening ocean in front of us. For two years I had walked this island every morning, but I had never stopped to watch the sunrise.

I was suddenly aware of the rough wooden box in my hand. *With this, we begin again*, I thought to myself. As we approached our home, I noticed that people were staring at us. No one spoke. To this day, I don't know why. Maybe it was because they felt as discouraged as I did. Or maybe it was because they somehow blamed me. Or maybe they simply didn't know what to say.

And then I saw him. There, sitting on a bench in front of my house, was Alessio. He was playing peacefully with Caesar, a white Persian cat that had stowed a ride back with me on a trip from Venice. For a moment I wondered if Alessio knew what had happened. In any case, he stood to embrace me.

After a few words, Alessio escorted me into the kitchen

and proceeded to concoct what he called the "perfect Venetian breakfast." Although he certainly never needed to cook for himself, Alessio considered cooking a form of art, and he fancied himself a great artist. In fact, he was. He had been asked on several occasions to prepare meals for leaders of state that frequently visited Venice. As Maria and I waited in the front room, Alessio banged and crashed his way around the kitchen, singing and laughing as he cooked.

How can he be this happy when I am so devastated? I thought to myself. *He must know something that I don't know.* I was right.

As we settled at a small table in a side room next to the kitchen, I realized that it had been many years since I had actually sat down for breakfast. Usually, I started my day on the docks and on the go. I smiled for the first time since the fire, as Alessio bounced into the room with a tray full of eggs and lamb and tomatoes. I wasn't the least bit hungry, but I forced myself to eat and chat with my friend. With my wife by my side and my cat under the table, I suddenly felt secure.

After the small talk had quieted, Alessio was first to broach the subject. "I heard about it from a good friend who was here last night, dropping off a shipment of tools. He wasn't more than a kilometer away when he saw the flames. He figured that the heat from the furnaces had ignited the wood of the building."

"Alessio, it was terrible. The flames caught so fast that half the building was gone before we could organize a rescue. We tried . . . we did all we could." I struggled to maintain my composure.

"I know, my friend. I knew that this would be a hard day to meet, but a deal is a deal. So I came to you." He smiled through his beard, now spotted with patches of gray.

For the first time, I noticed the wrinkles on the edges of his eyes, highlighting his constant smile and easy laugh. He was aging, but aging well. At fifty-five, he was still strong and smart. But time was beginning to take the edge off of his personality, which was a good thing for days like this.

"Thank you for coming," I said. It was the second time he had made the journey to Murano in the past year. He had surprised me and Maria on our wedding day. Unexpectedly, he showed up with a boat full of wedding presents, including four minstrels and an acrobatic group for entertainment. It was the highlight of our wedding. Now he was back. This time as an encourager . . . when we needed it the most.

As we finished the last of breakfast, Maria moved to the kitchen, and I was left alone with Alessio and Caesar. I struggled to speak but was determined to get the advice of my mentor. "What do I do now?" I asked.

"What do you mean?" Alessio replied.

"I mean, it's over. I've lost it all. I've got to find something new. In fact, all morning I've been thinking that maybe I should go back to the monastery. I mean, I couldn't live there, not with Maria. But maybe I could live somewhere nearby and work there. Alessio, I wonder if I might have missed my real calling."

"Why do you say that?"

"Well, it's obvious that God is closing a door in my business. Why else would He allow my factory to be burned?" For the first time that morning Alessio's face was serious. It was clear that he did not agree with me.

"Antonio, listen to me carefully. This might be the most important lesson that I teach you.

"Many men have robbed themselves of their destiny because they have allowed discouragement to rob them of their dreams."

"But, Alessio, I'm not only discouraged. I've failed!" For the first time, I could feel my patience with Alessio wearing thin. *How could he say that?* I thought.

"Antonio, remember that failure is not fatal unless you believe that it is. Consider this. Unless a butterfly pushes through its cocoon, it will die. Unless a chicken pushes through its egg, it will perish."

I nodded.

"Antonio, God is the Author of all that is good. He desires good things for us, not tragedy. But He always uses difficult times in our lives to prepare us for His greatness in us. Unless we struggle through trial, we will not become all that He wants us to become. Let me ask you, how are your glass beads made? I mean, what is the general process?"

"Well, the glass is heated and formed and then heated again and then—"

"Precisely. Unless the glass is subjected to the heat, it cannot achieve greatness. It is, in fact, the heat that prepared the glass for its final shape and color."

"I see. But maybe God is trying to tell me that He is closing a door in my life. Maybe He is trying to get my attention. Maybe He wants me back at the monastery."

"It's possible. But what's more probable is that God is preparing you for greatness. This may be one of the most important tests of your character that you'll ever encounter. Remember that one of the big misunderstandings we have of God is that when difficulty arises, He is closing a door. No. More often He is preparing you for something special. Remember this.

"TRIALS DEVELOP YOUR CHARACTER, PREPARING YOU FOR INCREASED BLESSINGS."

"So God allows failure so we—"

"God allows challenges, Antonio."

"Okay, God allows challenges so we can develop the character we need to accomplish His purpose for our lives?"

"Exactly. And not only that. He uses the challenges to make us stronger and more effective."

"Alessio, while we were fighting the fire I overheard several of our workers saying that the devil was destroying our building. To tell you the truth, I was starting to believe it myself. What do you think?"

"Well, Antonio, we often *mistakenly* give the enemy credit for things. Yes, it's true that he 'walks about like a roaring lion, seeking whom he may devour.' And he loves to attempt to kill us, steal from us, and destroy us."

"Then it must have been him!"

"Not so fast. Cause and effect probably has much more to do with what happened here last night than the enemy."

"Cause and effect?"

"Yes. We sometimes credit circumstances to God or the enemy, when really it is simple cause and effect. In your case, the cause and effect was the fact that you had several furnaces burning under the roof of a building that was built to hold maybe one or two. The heat from those furnaces probably was too intense for the roof, and eventually it caught on fire. That's not the devil at work. It's simple cause and effect."

I was a bit embarrassed, because I knew that Alessio was right. "I see. And I suppose that's my next lesson?"

"It is.

"TAKE RESPONSIBILITY FOR PROBLEMS THAT ARE THE RESULT OF YOUR OWN BAD DECISIONS. DON'T DISPLACE THE BLAME."

"So what do I do? I mean, how do I respond to these obstacles. I have no factory. I have no beads. I have no boats. I have no additional money."

"First, realize that what you are encountering are stepping stones, not obstacles. You can use this opportunity to strengthen your business, if you decide to."

"But how?"

"Didn't you tell me that you and Milos were planning on building a new factory soon?"

"Well, yes, but I—"

"Okay, then essentially you were already planning for this. It's just happened sooner than you'd hoped. And now, Antonio, you can use the loss of your factory as a catalyst for your greatest growth. It's your choice."

Julio jumped in, breaking the rhythm of the story. "What was the principle, Grandfather? What was the lesson that Alessio was trying to teach you?"

Antonio reached his hand down and flipped to the next page in the weathered book. The old pages flapped in the wind. Julio turned to watch. He slowly read the words.

PRINCIPLE SIX:
SEE CHALLENGES AS STEPPING
STONES, NOT AS OBSTACLES.

Julio was determined not to forget. He went back and reviewed the lessons of the journal . . .

PRINCIPLE ONE:
WORK HARD AND GOD WILL PROSPER YOU.

PRINCIPLE TWO:
FINANCIAL PROSPERITY IS OFTEN
CONNECTED TO SOUL PROSPERITY.

PRINCIPLE THREE:
A MAN MUST DO WHATEVER HE CAN
TO PROVIDE FOR HIS FAMILY.

PRINCIPLE FOUR:
TRIALS DEVELOP YOUR CHARACTER,
PREPARING YOU FOR INCREASED BLESSINGS.

PRINCIPLE FIVE:
TAKE RESPONSIBILITY FOR PROBLEMS
THAT ARE THE RESULT OF YOUR OWN BAD
DECISIONS. DON'T DISPLACE THE BLAME.

PRINCIPLE SIX:
SEE CHALLENGES AS STEPPING
STONES, NOT AS OBSTACLES.

The sun was now beginning to move back toward St. Peter's, and Julio realized that there were only a few precious hours left in the day. Antonio sighed deeply and looked Julio in the eyes.

"That year Milos and I worked hard to rebuild the factory. To our surprise, several of our largest customers sent workers to help. Within a few weeks a new factory was completed. Our business grew more during the next twelve months than it had since I started it six years before. It was true. The challenges had made me a better person. I was blessed with a bigger business, more employees, and more challenges."

"Blessed with more challenges?"

"Yes, Julio. You see, I had learned to embrace challenges. And during the next three years I experienced many. I didn't know how to solve all of them. So I waited."

"What were you waiting for?"

"For my next meeting, of course. My next meeting with Alessio."

CHAPTER SEVEN

THE FOURTH MEETING

As I turned the corner of the canal, I knew that my meeting with Alessio would once again be significant. The dancing light from the overhanging buildings reminded me of the terror that I had experienced only three years earlier as the flames eating through my factory had lit up the island sky. But somehow all that seemed distant now. Once again, Alessio had been right. My greatest challenges had led to my greatest triumphs.

After the fire, I had rebuilt the factory and had met with several key merchants from China and Spain. They had all decided to use Venetian beads as their primary currency. Despite the tragedy, the idea was working. The additional business from the Orient and Spain pushed our island factory to full capacity, and by the end of the year Milos and I were considering construction again. Things were going well. Going well, that is, until Ahmad.

My mind suddenly snapped to a picture of the feared merchant-pirate, Ahmad. I could feel the hair on the back of my neck stand on end as my inner eyes focused on his face. His sharp cheekbones seemed to jut up toward his ears, almost creature-like. His piercing green eyes appeared like jade stone against his dark features. He had long black hair that was tied together near the middle of his back. It blended with his equally black beard. He was the most notorious merchant in history.

I had often heard tales about Ahmad on late evenings while working on the docks. Even Alessio himself had told me stories of the great desert merchant. Legend said that Ahmad was as strong as he was smart. According to several of the dockhands, he had once killed a crocodile with his bare hands. Apparently, he could be just as dangerous with men.

The stories surrounding Ahmad were colorful and mysterious. Many people didn't believe that he even existed. But Alessio said that he had once caught a glimpse of him during a trip to Egypt. I had wondered myself if this phantom-trader was real. But any doubt about the existence of Ahmad had been shattered. I had seen him with my own eyes.

During a visit to Casablanca a month before, a messenger came to my room at the inn one evening as the sun was setting. The boy was no older than sixteen, and when I opened my door I could see that he was shaking. It was as if he'd seen a ghost. In broken Greek, he explained to me that Ahmad had heard about the beads. And he informed me that the famed merchant wanted to meet with me . . . alone. The boy handed me a parchment with instructions written on it. He told me to walk to the balcony of my room and to look out over the river that ran into the Mediterranean.

The messenger then bolted out, practically tripping over himself. I turned toward the doors of the balcony. There was a sheer curtain covering its windows, and the fabric billowed out in the warm air. Through it I could make out the shape of a boat on the water. The ship was moving silently down the river, now only four hundred feet from my room. I apprehensively walked through the balcony doors.

The schooner was massive. It must have been two hundred

feet long and thirty feet wide. The bow rose up at least twenty feet into the air, with the face of a dragon ornately carved on its front. The sides of the boat were made of dark wooden planks sealed with a sort of tar and capped with an ornate wooden railing that spanned from the bow to the stern. I could see more than twenty oars protruding from somewhere inside.

Four masts held sails that stretched the width of the deck and went upward of seventy-five feet. The same face of a dragon that adorned the front of the boat was embroidered on the canvas fabric. I immediately knew what I was looking at. It was Ahmad's boat. He was known to use the sign of the dragon as his trademark.

I scanned the deck. I noticed several men scurrying about, moving boxes and working the sails. But there was no sign of Ahmad. And then I saw him.

He emerged moments before the boat crossed in front of my room. Ahmad was wearing a white cloth around his waist, decorated with what appeared to be gold trim on the edges. Nothing covered his chest except a gold medallion that hung around his neck. It was clear that he was indeed very muscular. I suddenly believed all the stories about crocodiles and men. He stood with his hands on the railing, staring directly toward the bank of the river. He wore gold bracelets on his wrists, and his fingers were clenched onto the wood, so that his veins seemed to stand out on his arms.

For a moment, my instincts told me to turn and run. It required all the courage in me to stand my ground. I took my place on my balcony and placed my hands on the stone railing, very much in the same position as Ahmad. He was now about two hundred feet from where I was. The encounter would be brief but close. In my hand I could feel the parchment that the messenger had given me. I wondered for a moment what it read. Was it an invitation to trade? Or maybe it was a threat. Or even worse, a death sentence.

Our eyes locked, and he moved his head for the first time. He did not smile. His eyes never left mine. In the light of the setting sun, his eyes were haunting. As the boat passed, he continued to look at me for another minute, and then he turned to step back into the belly of the dragon.

It was at that moment I realized my heart was racing. My breaths were short and shallow, and my hands were dripping sweat. I quickly reached down to unfold the parchment in my hands. The perspiration had begun to fade the fresh ink on the page. But I could still read the markings written in perfect Greek.

> *I have been watching you. It is now time for us to meet. Allow the moon to turn twice, and sail to the barrier island, near the coast of Morocco. Bring no one with you, or your fate will be sealed. I will tell you more then.*

The letter was secured with wax, stamped with the face of a dragon. I sat down on a small chair in my room and read the letter over again several times. *What does he want from me?* I thought as I paced the room that night. My mind was spinning, and I could hardly wait to leave the inn and return home to Maria. The next morning as I set sail, I was grateful for my upcoming meeting with Alessio. There would be just enough time to get his counsel before my scheduled meeting with Ahmad.

I shuddered as I recollected my encounter with the merchant-pirate. But I felt safe on the familiar canals of Venice. The summer night air was warm, and I could hear the sounds of children laughing somewhere off in the distance. I thought of my young son, Valentino, and I suddenly longed to hold him and listen to Maria sing him a lullaby. The moon over my head was shining with a deep yellow glow, and it seemed to hang so low that I was sure I could reach out and touch it. Suddenly, the sounds of the children laughing were replaced with the distinct sound of someone else laughing. It was a full, bellowing laugh . . . a laugh that I knew well. It was Alessio.

He was standing with several dockhands. Alessio's hands were moving wildly above his head, and I knew that he was telling another story. He saw my boat and dashed toward me, waving and shouting.

We embraced, and he helped me unload a special box from Morocco that he had asked me to bring. "A gift for the priest down the street," he had told me. "It's a new statue for the church." We then took our places in his house at the now-familiar wooden table. I noticed that there was a small charcoal burn spot on the top and what appeared to be wax had melted into one of the carvings.

"Dropped a candle," Alessio said.

I smiled. In a few moments a meal was in front of us. I told Alessio of all the things that had happened since we had last met. I told him about the rebuilding of the factory. I told him about the birth of Valentino, my son. I told him about the development of the new trade routes and about the house that Maria and I had built on the beach. We talked and laughed, and I suddenly realized that this man, this great merchant, had somewhere along the path of life become more than a mentor . . . he had become my friend.

I had almost forgotten about Ahmad when one of Alessio's men, a tall Grecian with long black hair, walked through the room. His black hair reminded me of the merchant-pirate of the sea, and I quieted for a moment.

"What is it, my friend?" Alessio said.

"Ahmad. It's about Ahmad."

Alessio thought I was jesting, so he played along. "Ah. The phantom of the sea. So you'd like to hear another story like the ones I told you on the docks?"

"No, Alessio. I've seen him."

Alessio sat up in his chair and looked into my eyes, searching for the truth. "You mean you've met Ahmad the Trader? Tell me, friend, what happened?"

I reached down into the pouch on my jacket and pulled out the small parchment, which was still folded. "He gave this to me while I was in Morocco. It was sent by a messenger."

I handed the paper to Alessio. He opened it carefully. He seemed especially interested in the wax seal.

"It's genuine," he said after a long pause. "How did it happen? How did he look?"

Alessio had dreamed of someday meeting Ahmad. He wanted to know all the details. For the next hour, I told him about the inn, the ship, and the man with the piercing eyes. When I finished, Alessio sat back in his seat and sighed.

"So now what do I do?" I asked.

"What do you mean? You meet with him, of course."

"Are you crazy? He's a phantom. A pirate. A killer! And besides, I'm not sure how I'd react if he tried anything." Allesio was aware that I had a reputation for aggressiveness in business. I was passionate about my goals. I always had been.

My assertiveness had admittedly gotten me into trouble, but it had also gotten me where I was.

"What are you afraid of?" Alessio said, smiling.

"Well, besides the fact that he seems to have a soft spot for crocodiles, I've been thinking . . ."

"Go on," said Alessio.

"Last month I went to the monastery to visit Felipo and several of my friends. And we talked late into the evening about the importance of meekness. The monks told me that to be aggressive in business was a mistake. After all, they told me, Jesus said that the meek will 'inherit the earth.'"

"Antonio, let me tell you something. What you have just described is another misunderstanding of the Scriptures. The monks are right. It's true that the meek will inherit the earth. And it's true that God wants us to be meek. But He wants us to be meek toward Him, not toward men."

"So are you saying that it's okay to be aggressive in business? Aggressive like Ahmad?"

"Well, I wouldn't take it that far. Certainly God wants us to be kind. But He has designed you the way He has for a reason. God wants you to live to please Him, more than to please people. You should focus on being meek before God but bold before men."

"So do you think that I should go ahead and meet with Ahmad?"

"Yes. Who knows what God might have in store for you? Meet with him and remain strong in what you believe. If you need to, be aggressive. That's how God made you. He'll direct you." Alessio reached out across the table and handed me back the parchment.

I had told Maria that if Alessio thought it was wise, I would head for Morocco right after my time with him. So I strapped an iron sword to my side, checked my direction with the stars overhead, and set out into the Mediterranean Sea. As my boat began to drift, I reached down and found the leather-bound book that held the secrets to my growing empire. I paused and then wrote down the latest lesson that I had learned.

❧

Julio was beaming with life. Pirates! Swords! Adventure! He couldn't believe it. His grandfather had instantly turned into a hero right before his eyes.

"Grandfather! Did that really happen?"

"Of course it did. That and more."

"I want to hear how the story with Ahmad ended. But first . . . Grandfather, what did you write? What principle did you learn during the fourth visit?"

Antonio opened the leather book again, and to Julio's surprise he saw a small piece of parchment attached to the page. It was attached with wax that was marked with the distinctive shape of a dragon. On the parchment, Julio could clearly see the word *Ahmad*. His jaw dropped open. Below the parchment he read the words:

PRINCIPLE SEVEN:
BE MEEK BEFORE GOD BUT BOLD BEFORE MEN.

"So what happened, Grandfather? What happened with Ahmad?"

"That, Julio, is a story I will never forget."

∞

My mind was racing. I had anchored my ship, and as I rowed the dinghy toward the island, I was sure that my wife would never hear from me again.

I saw the beach that Ahmad had described in the note, and I remembered the words of Alessio: "Be bold before men."

The moon was full, and the light reflected off the waves as they lapped against the sand. I could smell the salt in the air, mixed with the aroma of ripe durian fruit. I noticed several palm trees scattered on the beach. But no sign of Ahmad. As I neared the beach, I could feel my heart beating quickly.

I jumped into the water moments before my boat scooted up onto the sand. I anchored the bow to a nearby driftwood log and scanned the beach. Nothing but the swaying of palm trees. My pulse was slowing, and I was beginning to think that I had been the victim of a practical joke. And then I saw him.

He seemed to appear from nowhere. Ahmad was standing no more than fifty feet from me. I was suddenly nervous. I imagined jumping into my boat and heading back to Murano. "Be bold before men," I said to myself.

And I stepped forward.

I moved steadily toward Ahmad, but he didn't move. When I was four feet from him, I extended my hand. I was breathing quickly, and for a moment I wondered if he would reach for the sword hanging precariously at his side. To my relief, he thrust his hand out to meet mine. Our words that night on the beach were few but meaningful.

"I am expanding my trade across the sea, and I am in need of a new currency of exchange. I was given these by a friend." Ahmad held out his hand to reveal five Venetian trading beads.

"I'd like to use these. It's my desire to establish an arrangement with you to provide my fleet with trading beads."

His words spun through my head, and I wondered for a moment if I had heard him correctly. "Do you mean you would like to purchase my beads as currency for your trading business?" I asked, just to be sure.

Ahmad smiled for the first time, his white teeth beaming through his dark features. "Yes, I would. And by the way, I apologize for the unusual arrangements of this meeting. The walls in Casablanca have ears. As my trading business has grown, I have made many new friends . . . and a few enemies as well. The efficiency of my operations and the speed of my ships have enabled me to offer a better product at a significantly lower price than my competitors."

"And so that's the reason you selected this deserted island?" I asked. I was suddenly seeing a different person than the legends had portrayed. This was not a fierce man at all, but rather one who was smart and articulate. My admiration for Ahmad grew as we walked the beach that evening, discussing the possibilities of trading together.

As I sailed away from the island the next morning, I listened to the sound of the surf crashing against the sand, and Alessio's words echoed through my mind. *Be bold before men.* I thanked my friend silently for his advice as I waved good-bye to Ahmad and headed back to my ship.

And with that, trade with Africa, India, Egypt, and other lands across the sea opened up to me. I frequently accompanied

Ahmad along the coast of Africa and even into Asia. Within several years my dream for a universal currency had become a reality. My business grew beyond my greatest expectations, and I was quickly becoming known as one of the most influential merchants in the world.

CHAPTER EIGHT

THE FIFTH MEETING

It was April and a breeze was blowing from the north, cooling the two as they sat on the steps of the great cathedral. Julio noticed for the first time the way the sun was gleaming off of the giant dome that hung over the main structure of St. Peter's. The reflections of light danced on the plaza in flowing arches. Julio was full of images of his Grandfather and Alessio and the mysterious Ahmad. He was eager for more.

"Grandfather, what happened next?"

∽

The ordeal with Ahmad had been challenging, but I'd learned some valuable lessons. Soon, though, I was dealing with a different kind of problem. It began with the youngest of Maria's brothers, whom she had nicknamed Venny. Maria had four brothers, all older than she was. Growing up in a family of boys had been an adventure, but Maria often said she'd have it no other way. She had fond memories of playing sport and fishing right along with them. Maria's father was a struggling merchant on Murano, and his boys had followed in his footsteps. Each had his own business, except for Venny. At twenty-one, he had spent most of his time fishing and painting. One day, in keeping with family tradition, Venny announced that he would open a restaurant.

I can still remember it. He sat down with me to discuss his plans. His eyes were full of life and adventure. I recognized the look on his face. After all, I'd been living a business adventure of my own. A few months later, he launched his first restaurant. Like any new enterprise, the first two years were difficult ones. Venny worked hard and slowly grew his small business. Unfortunately, his debt also grew. Soon, he found himself desperate for money, wondering what to do. That's when I heard the knock at my door.

I had just finished writing letters to several of my key customers when he arrived. When I saw that it was Venny, I quickly opened the door and invited him in. Immediately, I could see a nervous look on his face. I offered him a cup of hot tea, and we sat down together in a room overlooking the ocean. After we settled in with small talk, he began to unravel the events of the past two years. He told me about his lack of start-up capital and about the employees who had stolen from his business. After only two years, he had found himself in debt and financially out of control. I remember asking him if there was anything I could do for him. I also remember the long pause. Then he asked me.

"Antonio, I would never normally do this . . . but what I really need right now is money. Is there any way that you could give me a loan? Just to get me through this."

I wanted to loan him money to help him through this difficult season. But I had some reticence. I told Venny that I needed to seek counsel before I made a commitment.

Venny's reaction was less than positive. He accused me of being selfish with my money. I remember watching him walk away from my house. I wanted desperately to help him, but I was unsure how.

As I moved down the canal recounting the events of the previous day, I was grateful that I would be able to get Alessio's counsel before making a decision. This would be our fifth session. One and a half decades had passed since I had first met with him.

"Antonio! Antonio! You've missed the docks!"

The shouts woke me from my reverie, and I realized that I had rowed right past Alessio's house. I looked back in the direction of his voice and saw him standing at the end of his dock waving his hands wildly over his head.

"Antonio, pull aside on the next canal! At the dock near the church!"

I nodded at Alessio and made a quick turn. As I neared the church and the dock, I looped the thick rope around my hand and stood on the small ledge on the bow of my boat. I noticed that the dock was already filled with other boats of various sizes, and I quickly scanned the slips for a place to land. I nearly had passed by when I noticed a small opening, just big enough to hold my boat. With the precision of a seasoned deckhand, I steered into the spot, jumped from the boat, and quickly tied it to the pier.

As I turned toward the church and the road leading to Alessio's house, I saw the resident priest. He was pacing behind the church, apparently praying before the midnight mass. As I approached, I received the same glare that he had given Alessio years before. I had learned my lesson and returned his look with a pleasant smile.

I walked in silence down the dusty road from the church toward Alessio's house. It would take at least ten minutes, but I didn't mind. The air was warm and the sky was clear. I identified some stars above my head that were shaped like a soup dipper. I quickly spotted the North Star, and I was reminded of the many times it had helped guide me back to Venice. As I was looking up at the sky, I suddenly bumped into what felt like the trunk of a tree. With a *whack* I toppled backward, and I had to skillfully maneuver to avoid falling. *What did I hit?* I thought to myself. But then the sound of laughter gave it away.

"You've got to watch where you're going," a voice shouted. I knew it was him. Before I could say anything, Alessio's strong arms grabbed my shoulders.

"My friend, it's good to see you again! You're looking as healthy as ever," I responded. And he was, even though the hair of his beard was now completely gray and the subtle wrinkles on his face had become more defined. As we walked, I told him about my new partnership with Ahmad and about the expansion of my business.

We arrived at his house just in time to see the cook place the evening meal on the table. The smell of fresh pasta and tomatoes caused my stomach to churn and my mouth to water. We quickly sat down and blessed the food, and I then finished telling him about the last three years.

Alessio smiled, but said little. "What are your plans for the coming year, Antonio?" he asked me.

"I'll expand again," I replied. "The demand for beads has been greater than ever. I've already talked to Milos about building a second factory."

Alessio nodded. He knew there was more on my mind. "What's bothering you, Antonio?" he asked.

Neither of us said anything for a moment. Finally, I broke the silence. "Just before I left on this trip I had an argument with Maria's brother. He accused me of hoarding my money."

"Why did he say that?" asked Alessio.

"Because I was hesitating about his request for a loan."

"And why did he want a loan?" pursued Alessio.

"He's started a new business, and he's overextended himself. Now he's in trouble financially. I certainly have the money. I should probably loan it to him."

"And what happens if he can't pay you as you agreed?" queried Alessio.

"I don't really know."

"I'll tell you what will happen. Your relationship with your brother-in-law will be hurt, and possibly your relationship with Maria. Loaning money damages relationships. And in this case, if you give him the money, because he hasn't changed his bad money-management style, it's only a matter of time before he's in trouble again. Antonio, it is important that you take this opportunity to teach your brother-in-law some principles that will help him in the future.

"First, avoid debt. Scripture says, 'Owe no one anything except to love one another.' That means that you owe love to all of God's children, but you are never to owe money. If you want to buy something but don't have the money for it, you don't buy it. Secondly, live below your means. You see, God honors delayed gratification."

∽

Julio looked down at the journal in his hands, and as he turned the page, he read:

PRINCIPLE EIGHT:
LIVE DEBT-FREE AND BELOW YOUR MEANS.

Julio paused for a moment. "But how do you form the habit of living below your means, Grandfather?"

"Julio, Alessio told me that since he was a young man he had developed a habit of creating a monthly budget of his income and expenses. Since that day, I've lived my life and I've grown my business by always staying within a budget."

Julio interrupted. "Grandfather, how did you create a budget? What does one look like?"

Antonio reached down and turned the page of the journal to reveal the inscription of the next principle along with what appeared to be a table of numbers with a large T in the middle, dividing the two columns. Antonio recited the next principle as Julio read it.

PRINCIPLE NINE:
ALWAYS KEEP TO YOUR BUDGET.

On the heading of one column was written the word *expenses*, and on the top of the other column was the word *income*. Under the *expense* listing were things like food, rent, and boat repairs. Under the *income* column were listings like wages and money from other sources.

"This was the first budget that I ever prepared. It was after my meeting with Alessio. On my return home, I helped Venito do the same thing."

Julio interrupted. "Venito? Wasn't that the name of the restaurant owner where we had lunch a few hours ago?"

"Yes, that's him."

"You mean *Venny* is *Venito*? He's your brother-in-law? Grandmother Maria's brother?" Julio was beginning to put the pieces together. "But he's got a successful restaurant. He said he had nine of them. I'm a little confused . . ."

"Well, at first Venito wasn't very receptive to my advice. He and Maria had grown up in a poor family, and his father had to work hard for the little they had. He actually resented Maria and me for our wealth, and it made it difficult for him to accept the fact that I had declined him the loan. But after a while, he came back and asked me for my advice, not my money. I was able to share with him the principles that I have just shared with you. And he used the principles to open nine restaurants, four of them here in Rome."

Julio smiled as everything began to fit together in his mind. He turned the page and read the words out loud:

PRINCIPLE TEN:
LOANING MONEY DESTROYS RELATIONSHIPS.

"Like in the story of you and Great-Uncle Venny, right?" Julio asked.

"That's right. Thankfully, I learned this from Alessio before it cost me valuable relationships."

"Grandfather, thank you for teaching me these lessons in handling my money. Of course, I don't have much yet, but when I do I'll know how to manage it better."

"That's not all, Julio," said Antonio.

"Not all? What do you mean?" Julio asked.

"Well, I've saved the most important money principle for last. Turn to the next page."

Julio turned the page of the journal, and he noticed that instead of text, charts were drawn onto the pages. He immediately saw several more large Ts, and realized that they all had something in common. At the top of each one was written, "10 percent GOD." "What does that mean, Grandfather?"

"Every month I have made it a habit to give to God the first 10 percent of my income. It's a scriptural principle, and I believe that God has blessed me for it."

"You see, it's critical that you understand that everything you have—your life, your friends, your health, and your money—are all gifts from God. It's important to sow 10 per-cent of your income back to God to honor Him. It's only after a farmer sows seed that he can reap a harvest."

Julio read the principle silently.

PRINCIPLE ELEVEN:
SET ASIDE THE FIRST 10 PERCENT TO HONOR GOD.

For a moment, the two sat without saying a word.

Then Antonio reached over and grabbed his grandson's hands. "Julio, remember to learn to control your money before it controls you."

"I understand, Grandfather." Julio sat silently for a few more moments . . . just thinking.

CHAPTER NINE

THE SIXTH
MEETING

I received the letter a few days before our final meeting," Antonio said with a twinkle in his eyes. "A letter? What letter?" asked Julio. The sun was beginning to set over the colonnades of the great piazza in front of St. Peter's. Julio squinted to see his grandfather's face in the light of the setting sun behind him. He realized for the first time that the streets were now nearly deserted, except for the occasional monk headed in the direction of the basilica.

"Come, Julio. I want to finish this story. But I want you to see the sunset from the steps of the great cathedral."

"Grandfather, I know that you've been here before. To the cathedral, I mean. But why did you want to take me *here* for this teaching?"

As Julio stood to his feet, Antonio had already moved from the table and was beginning to walk in the direction of the church. Julio looked down and saw the leather-bound journal still lying there, open. He reached down and placed it carefully under his arm.

"Grandfather, you left this . . ."

"It's yours now," Antonio said with a gleam in his eye.

"But, Grandfather, I couldn't."

"Julio, I've lived my life according to the principles in that book. Now I want you to have it."

"But, Grandfather, don't you want to keep it somewhere important and safe?"

"Yes, I do, Julio. There could be no safer place than in your heart. You see, if you will take this book and learn the principles written in it, your life will be changed too. I want you to have this journal, read the life principles in it, and determine to live by them. If you do, your success will be greater than you could ever imagine."

Julio felt as though he had just received a king's treasure. As they approached the colonnades, he tucked the book under his arm and proudly walked up the steps leading into the great plaza.

"Julio, one of the most important lessons Alessio taught me was the necessity of giving to others the lessons that you have learned yourself."

They were about halfway back across the great plaza and had just passed one of the fountains when a group of young monks moved in quickly from behind them. It was apparent that they were on their way to a class or lecture of some sort. Each had a book in his hand, and they were all walking behind one particular monk who seemed to be leading the way. The monks were dressed in gray robes, tied at the waist with thick white ropes. Large hoods were draped across their shoulders.

Antonio's mind raced quickly back to his time at the monastery where he'd spent so much of his youth. He remembered his friends, the monks. He remembered their laughter at suppertime. He remembered the power of their prayers in the morning and their deep sincerity of worship during mass.

As the monks passed, a million pictures flashed in front of him. Pictures of fields that gleamed golden at the end of a long day. Pictures of the small church where they would worship and pray. Antonio's heart pulsed with a sudden love for his ministry friends, the faithful men who had given their lives to serve God. Then he thought of his good friend Alessio, and tears welled up as he remembered how he . . . .

"Grandfather, should we sit here . . . on the steps?" Julio's voice jolted Antonio back to reality, and he realized that they were now standing at the same place where the story had begun only a few hours earlier.

"Yes, let's sit here together," responded Antonio. "I remember the last time I met with Alessio . . ."

∽

The gardens of Murano are known for their beauty, and ours was no exception. I was in the garden with Maria when the messenger arrived. Maria and I had been sitting, watching the sun set on the water for what had seemed like hours.

As we stood to return to the house, we saw him waiting at the entrance to our garden. He was a young man, maybe eighteen, with bright red hair and strong features. He was very out of place for Venice, and I figured that he was probably Gaelic. It wasn't entirely out of the ordinary to see a stranger at our house. We often entertained business guests from as far away as the Orient. I walked over to greet the young man, who extended his hand first.

"A pleasure to meet you, Mr. Antonio. I have heard so much about you and your enterprise on Murano."

"You have heard about me? And to whom do I owe the gratitude of my introduction?" I replied.

"Alessio, the merchant, sir. I have been in his employ for several months, and he has sent me here to bring you this letter." With that, the young man reached down into a brown leather satchel by his side and retrieved a small envelope. He presented it to me, and I turned it over in my hands. Yes, it was certainly from Alessio. But there was a strange seal carefully placed over its edges. I looked closer and quickly recognized that it was the seal of the Vatican. It appeared to be the seal of the pope himself. It couldn't be . . .

"I've been instructed to bring you this letter, and then to return immediately to Mr. Alessio." The young man seemed a bit anxious. So I resisted the temptation of questioning him further and released him to return back to Venice.

Maria was now at my side, and she smiled as she too realized who the letter was from. The handwriting on the front of the letter was Alessio's. It said, "To My Trusted Friend, Antonio." I quickly turned the envelope over and pushed my finger against the seal to break it.

∽

Julio interrupted, "Grandfather, do you still have the letter?" He fumbled through *The Journal of a King* and found a yellowed sheet of paper wedged carefully between two pages. "Is this the one?" He held the nearly illegible parchment in his hands.

Antonio nodded, and Julio slowly opened the letter. The writing was faded and somewhat broken, but he could still make out the scrawling on the inside:

Dearest Antonio,

Greetings, my friend. I trust that this letter finds you healthy and well. Next week marks the eighteenth year of our kindred friendship. As we have agreed, we will meet again, just as we have for many years. But this will be our last meeting, and I have made special arrangements. This year, we will not meet in Venice, but in the great city of Rome. I want to show you something. Follow the instructions written below. I will be waiting. God's speed.

Your Friend,
Alessio

"In Rome? But why?" wondered Julio. Antonio smiled as he continued the story.

∞

I quickly refolded the letter and glanced at Maria. "Rome?"

She shrugged and gently placed her arm in mine while we walked together toward the house. "You must leave soon if you are to arrive on time," she said as the sun disappeared over the horizon. "I'll prepare your things."

After a restless night's sleep, I mobilized my crew. We made our way through the lagoons of Murano and into the open sea. It was only ten o'clock in the morning, but the Mediterranean sun beat down on us as we worked to catch the wind in our sails. The Adriatic was unusually calm. Several times we slowed to a near standstill, making our way around the boot of the mainland and back up toward the Tiber River and the banks of Rome.

Like Venice, the coast at the mouth of the Tiber River had become a sort of focal point for world trade. Merchant ships congested the shipping lanes as traffic converged from Asia, Africa, and Western Europe.

Heading upstream, the wind suddenly picked up, and I could feel the strength of my boat push against the current. Within a few hours I began to see the signs of Rome, towering relics of a distant empire combined with shining emblems of a new era. I glanced down at Alessio's letter and searched the banks for the Castel Saint Angelo, the home of the Vatican leaders. It didn't take long for me to find it. A gigantic cylindrical edifice jutted from the ground and towered majestically over the river. The building was protected by walls that were flanked by great statues celebrating the glory of God and Rome. I remembered that this was the very fortress that Pope Boniface IX had used to protect Rome against attack seventy-five years earlier.

Alessio had given me instructions. I was to secure my boat and then follow the directions to find him. The Roman docks were packed with people. People loading and unloading, buying and selling. The stagnant smell on the docks was a combination of perspiration and fish.

I found the road that I had been instructed to follow, and I began my trek. I calculated that I'd be walking for at least another hour, so I stopped briefly to refresh myself. I sat down at a café near the market and watched the bustling economy of Rome unfold before me. An older woman sat at a table across from me, and I couldn't help but notice the ornate gold cross around her neck. She nodded to me as I stood to walk the final distance.

The grand buildings of Rome towered around me, and I wondered where Alessio was taking me. Alessio had mentioned a church . . . a grand church. I pictured St. Mark's Basilica in Venice. That was my landmark . . . a grand church. I supposed I must be getting close, because groups of monks were now filling the street.

I pressed on up a hill. My small pack suddenly seemed to weigh a hundred pounds. I began to wonder if I'd taken a wrong turn, when suddenly I realized where I was. St. Peter's.

At first, I wasn't sure what to think. It appeared that the place where the great cathedral had been built was now completely in ruins. I shook my head in sudden confusion, and then I remembered the conversations with the monks at the monastery. They had told me of the plans to demolish the old church that had been originally built by Constantine. It was to be replaced with a new, grander church. They had explained that the original cathedral had fallen into disrepair and that funds could not be raised to restore it properly.

∽∽∽

"Wait, Grandfather! Do you mean *this* St. Peter's? Do you mean you visited here before the basilica was ever built?" exclaimed Julio in surprise.

"Yes, Julio. I was here. In fact, I was standing on a small hill just about where we're sitting right now."

"What about the old church? What about the old St. Peter's?"

"Well, the original cathedral's altar was placed directly over the spot where St. Peter's bones were buried."

"Really? St. Peter, himself, was actually here?"

"Oh yes, he most certainly was. And for over fifteen hundred years people have visited this place from all over the world to worship God and to remember the great work of St. Peter."

Julio took a deep breath as he struggled to take it all in. Then he remembered Alessio. "Grandfather, what happened to Alessio? Wasn't he supposed to meet you for your last visit?"

"Ah, yes. Alessio knew that I'd walk toward the burial place of St. Peter, and he sent a messenger to meet me."

∽∽∽

The sun was directly over Vatican hill. I quickly looked around, hoping to find Alessio. But there were dozens of workers, architects, and priests sprawled out across the place, surveying the area for the new building. I suddenly felt a hand on my shoulder. I spun around to find the same red-haired young man whom I had met only a week before in my garden.

"Alessio is waiting," he said with a smile.

I simply followed, not knowing what to say. An elderly monk greeted us at the door of a small building next to the ruins, and he led us down a dimly lit corridor. As we walked in silence down the hallway, I imagined that the Emperor Constantine himself might have used this same torch-lit path. The monk stopped in front of a wooden door no more than five feet high with four-inch steel bands stretching around it in three places.

"Open it when you're ready. He's expecting you." And with that, the monk and the red-haired man returned quietly back along the hallway. I found myself oddly alone, staring solemnly at the oak door. *I wonder what this year will bring?* I thought, reaching down to pull the black iron handle.

The door creaked and moaned as it slowly opened. I could see another torch flickering in the room. The rest of the chamber was out of my sight because the door was so low. I ducked and slowly walked in.

It took a moment for my eyes to adjust in the dim light. The room was about fifteen feet long and ten feet wide. The center of one wall had what appeared to be a window that was covered by a canvas. Across, on another wall, was a small washbasin and bathing area. Besides that, the room was bare, except for the bed that was situated directly under the canvas. As my eyes acclimated, I noticed Alessio standing there in a shadowy corner.

"My friend, I've been expecting you. Come, Antonio. Here is a chair." His voice was frail and weak. "I'm afraid I have no dinner to offer you this time. But today we have important business."

I was concerned as I walked toward my old friend. It was as though Alessio had aged twenty years in only three. His face was weathered and crossed with lines. What was left of his hair was thin and sparse. His breathing was labored and sporadic. *Could this be the same man?* I thought to myself. I could feel my throat tightening and fought to keep my eyes from watering as I eased into the chair by his side. Suddenly I realized that it wasn't Alessio that needed the comfort; it was me. No sooner had the thought crossed my mind than I felt his steady hand take mine.

"Antonio, this is not a time for worry. This is a time for action." Suddenly his voice punched with the same vigor that it had for eighteen years.

"Remember, Antonio, every day is a gift from God. We must use each one wisely. Now, this is our final meeting together, and the life lesson of today is the most important one that I will give you." Alessio strained to look me directly in the eyes.

"Antonio, you have done well. You have followed your passion and built a great empire to the glory of God. You have used your gifts and talents to serve people and to extend the reach of your influence. Now it is time for you to reach up."

"Reach up? I don't understand."

"Antonio, you have been blessed by the hand of God because you have been faithful with what He has given you. Now it is important that you use what you have learned and earned to glorify Him further."

"But how, Alessio?"

"Antonio, do you remember the conversations that I had with your father, Felipo? The conversations about how God has made us kings and priests?"

"Yes. I remember. But how does that apply now?"

"Antonio, God has designed a special relationship between businessmen and leaders in the church. We, as businessmen, can provide the provision for the vision of the priests."

"Alessio, I am always willing to obey God. He has blessed me greatly. What can I do?"

With that, Alessio reached up and with all his strength pulled the canvas away from his window. The room burst with light. I flinched and moved my hands in front of my eyes. After a time, as I lowered my hands, I could see a panoramic view of the location of the old St. Peter's. Men with axes and shovels and other tools were carefully working to prepare the foundation of the new building.

"Antonio, this has been my passion for the past eighteen years. I knew that God desired to be honored in this place, and I wanted to do everything I could to help restore the glory back to St. Peter's. As it has turned out, we had to demolish the old building to make way for the new one. That has been my role. Every year I have spent time in this room, and I have given money to see that the old building was removed and that a new foundation was put into place. It has been a long process. But now it is ready. And it will be the most magnificent cathedral ever built to the Glory of God." Alessio's eyes were glossy, and his voice was broken as he spoke.

"But now, my part is nearly over. I have given all that I can give. My health is leaving me, and my fortune has now been given to my family. Antonio, you can carry on this work, if you choose."

"But I—"

"Not now. I simply wanted to share with you a living picture of the final lesson."

❧

Julio was reading from the journal.

PRINCIPLE TWELVE:
UNDERSTAND THE POWER OF PARTNERSHIP.

Antonio smiled. "Yes, Julio. That day I learned the power of partnership. The power of the partnership between the laity and the clergy. The power of the partnership between the kings and the priests. You see, there is a tugging on the hearts of every one of us to have a closer relationship with God. And there is a craving in every one of us to do whatever we can to further His kingdom. Well, one way we can do that is by partnering with the priests who have been given a vision by God. We provide the provision to see that the vision is fulfilled."

"So what did you do, Grandfather? Did *you* build St. Peter's?"

"No, not exactly. It took many men to build this cathedral. But because of my relationship with Alessio, I was able to meet with the pope myself. And I was blessed to be able to partner with him to help finance the construction of this wonderful church."

Julio could hardly believe it. He suddenly realized the power of the ideas in the book in his hands, and he carefully closed the cover. He ran the twelve principles of the journal through his memory one more time:

PRINCIPLE ONE:
WORK HARD AND GOD WILL PROSPER YOU.

PRINCIPLE TWO:
FINANCIAL PROSPERITY IS OFTEN
CONNECTED TO SOUL PROSPERITY.

PRINCIPLE THREE:
A MAN MUST DO WHATEVER HE CAN
TO PROVIDE FOR HIS FAMILY.

PRINCIPLE FOUR:
TRIALS DEVELOP YOUR CHARACTER,
PREPARING YOU FOR INCREASED BLESSINGS.

PRINCIPLE FIVE:
TAKE RESPONSIBILITY FOR PROBLEMS
THAT ARE THE RESULT OF YOUR OWN BAD
DECISIONS. DON'T DISPLACE THE BLAME.

PRINCIPLE SIX:
SEE CHALLENGES AS STEPPING
STONES, NOT AS OBSTACLES.

PRINCIPLE SEVEN:
BE MEEK BEFORE GOD BUT BOLD BEFORE MEN.

PRINCIPLE EIGHT:
LIVE DEBT-FREE AND BELOW YOUR MEANS.

PRINCIPLE NINE:
ALWAYS KEEP TO YOUR BUDGET.

PRINCIPLE TEN:
LOANING MONEY DESTROYS RELATIONSHIPS.

PRINCIPLE ELEVEN:
SET ASIDE THE FIRST 10 PERCENT TO HONOR GOD.

PRINCIPLE TWELVE:
UNDERSTAND THE POWER OF PARTNERSHIP.

"Grandfather, thank you for bringing me here today. Thank you for sharing the ideas that have made you successful. And thank you for giving me this treasure."

As the sun crept behind the colonnades surrounding the plaza, Antonio smiled and stood to his feet. "Oh, there is one condition to your keeping the book, Julio."

"What is it, Grandfather? I'll do anything."

"Next year. You are to be here on the steps of this cathedral . . . in one year."

"Will I meet with you, Grandfather?"

"You'll see. In one year someone will be here to meet with you."

And with that, Antonio and Julio walked across the greatest plaza of the greatest cathedral in the world. As they stepped into the shadows of the columns, another perfect Vatican day was ending. But the legend of the monk and the merchant was only just beginning.

NOTE TO THE READER

Just as Antonio passed on the Twelve Keys to Successful Living, it is now your turn to share *The Journal of a King* with others.

SCRIPTURE REFERENCES

STUDY
GUIDE

The following study guide is suitable for individuals or small groups. It is divided into twelve sessions and loosely follows the chronology of the book. Each session contains material that expands on a particular theme found in *The Legend of the Monk and the Merchant*, including biblical support, and ends with a series of questions that can be contemplated privately or discussed in a group. You are invited to take notes on the blank pages at the back of the book. Please read *The Legend of the Monk and the Merchant* in its entirety before beginning.

THE INACCURATE DIVISION BETWEEN THE MONK AND THE MERCHANT, BETWEEN CLERGY AND LAITY

In his book *Marketplace Christianity*, Robert Fraser observes,

> Modern Christian heroes are vocational ministers: Rees Howells, David Brainerd, George Muller, Charles Wesley, Finney, Jonathan Edwards, John Calvin, Smith Wigglesworth, Mother Teresa—the list goes on.
>
> In contrast, most biblical heroes *were not priests*. Abraham was a rancher and a businessman; Joseph was a businessman and a skilled administrator. Joshua and Caleb were generals; David was a shepherd, a general, and a king; Daniel and Nehemiah were governmental administrators. But these biblical heroes have been interpreted for us

through the eyes of modern-day priests and they have been stripped of their marketplace identity.[1]

At the cathedral, Felipo shares with Alessio an important Bible verse: Revelation 1:6, which says Jesus "has made us kings and priests to His God and Father." Note that *has made* is a continuing verb, so a more accurate understanding of the verse is "continues to make us kings and priests."

One of the twelve tribes of Israel was the tribe of Levi. Under the old covenant, the Levites were set apart as a tribe of priests to serve God (Numbers 3:5–10). All eleven other tribes were required to go through the Levites to worship and make sacrifices. But under the new covenant, because all Christians now have the Holy Spirit, all believers are priests and can personally worship God and minister to God and his people:

> "Nevertheless I tell you the truth. It is to your advantage that I go away; for if I do not go away, the Helper will not come to you; but if I depart, I will send Him to you." (John 16:7)

> You also, as living stones, are being built up a spiritual house, a holy priesthood, to offer up spiritual sacrifices acceptable to God through Jesus Christ. (1 Peter 2:5)

> But you are a chosen generation, a royal priesthood, a holy nation, His own special people, that you may proclaim the

praises of Him who called you out of darkness into His marvelous light. (1 Peter 2:9)

And He Himself gave some to be apostles, some prophets, some evangelists, and some pastors and teachers, for the equipping of the saints for the work of ministry, for the edifying of the body of Christ. (Ephesians 4:11–12)

All Christians are to be in ministry. All are considered by God to be priests. Some are in vocational ministry (receiving a salary for their ministry) and some are in ministry in marketplace venues (not receiving a salary for their ministry).

But whether in vocational ministry (monks) or ministry in the marketplace (merchants), we are all called to "go therefore and make disciples of all the nations, baptizing them in the name of the Father and of the Son and of the Holy Spirit, teaching them to observe all things that [Jesus has] commanded you" (Matthew 28:19–20).

This command by Jesus is known as the Great Commission, and it falls upon all believers because all Christians are priests and are in ministry. Christianity is not a spectator sport where the congregation (what has been called *the laity*) watches the vocational ministers (what have been called *the clergy*) do the work of the ministry.

Revelation 1:6 also says that we are all "kings" as well as "priests." A king is someone who has authority and influence over a group of people. You've heard it said that a man's home is his castle; he is the king of the castle and its inhabitants, his family. A woman is a "kingette" over her children. You might be in a position of authority over a group of people in the workplace or might have influence over people at your children's school or in your neighborhood. Even people in vocational ministry are kings, having influence outside of their religious world.

In the foreword, Dave Ramsey talks about how reading *The Legend of the Monk and the Merchant* clarified his thoughts on the false conflict between church and commerce:

> Author Terry Felber helped me put the whole church/business debate in a new light. I was finally able to express that the monk is holy—*and so is the merchant!* What the merchant does *is a ministry*.... We're not called to separate our spiritual life from our work life, and we're not called to divide our Sunday morning worship from our Monday morning staff meetings. God is in both, and He blesses both....
>
> Everyone in [our] building knows that they're operating under a higher calling, *because our work is holy.*

Charles Spurgeon echoes Ramsey's realization that we all engage in ministry, regardless of our employment: "Any Christian has a right to disseminate the gospel who has the ability to do so; and more, he not only has the right, but it is his duty to do so as long as he lives. . . . The propagation of the gospel is left, not to a few, but to all the disciples of the Lord Jesus Christ."[2]

Many countries that are closed to Christian missionaries welcome American business opportunities. So when we take into account ministry in the marketplace, there is really no such thing as a country that is closed to the gospel.

Discussion

- Have you held an inaccurate paradigm, separating the clergy and the laity? Have you put people in vocational ministry on a pedestal, thinking they have a closer connection with God? Why?

- Have you been fulfilling your roles as king and priest? Where are you a king with influence? What venue has God given you for ministry?

- How do you see yourself fulfilling the Great Commission talked about in Matthew 28:19–20?

- What does Spurgeon's statement say about your call to ministry?

- Which call do you think is more rewarding, vocational ministry or marketplace ministry? Why?

CALLED TO OPERATE PRIMARILY OUTSIDE THE MEETING PLACE

ecall Jesus' Great Commission (Matthew 28:19–20): "Go therefore and make disciples of all the nations, baptizing them in the name of the Father and of the Son and of the Holy Spirit, teaching them to observe all things that I have commanded you." If we dissect this scripture passage, we see that the first word, *go*, in the original Greek is *poreuomai*, which means "depart." So a believer is to leave the place where he is currently located and depart to another location. In other words, Christians are to leave their places of fellowship, the four walls of the church. Where are they to depart to?

And Jesus answered and spoke to them again by parables and said: "The kingdom of heaven is like a certain king who arranged a marriage for his son, and sent out his servants to call those who were invited to the wedding; and they were not willing to come. Again, he sent out other servants, saying, 'Tell those who are invited, "See, I have prepared my dinner; my oxen and fatted cattle are killed, and all things are ready. Come to the wedding."' But they made light of it and went their ways, one to his own farm, another to his business. And the rest seized his servants, treated them spitefully, and killed them. But when the king heard about it, he was furious. And he sent out his armies, destroyed those murderers, and burned up their city. Then he said to his servants, 'The wedding is ready, but those who were invited were not worthy. Therefore *go into the highways, and as many as you find, invite to the wedding.* So those servants went out into the highways and gathered together all whom they found, both bad and good. And the wedding hall was filled with guests.

"But when the king came in to see the guests, he saw a man there who did not have on a wedding garment. So he said to him, 'Friend, how did you come in here without a wedding garment?' And he was speechless. Then the king said to the servants, 'Bind him hand and foot, take him away, and cast him into outer darkness; there will be weeping and gnashing of teeth.'" (Matthew 22:1–13, emphasis added)

In this parable, the king (meaning God the Father) tells

the servants (meaning Christians who have confessed Jesus as their Lord [Romans 10:9]) to "go into the highways." The word *go*, meaning "depart," is the same Greek word used in Matthew 28:19. Where are Jesus' servants to depart to? *The highways.* That doesn't sound like the four walls of the church. What are they to do in the highways? *Invite people to the wedding.*

The church, or body of believers, is pictured in Scripture as the bride of Christ (John 3:29). The parable illustrates that when God the Father, the king, appears at the wedding feast, those who are not clothed properly in Him will be cast into outer darkness.

Our job then, as God's servants, is to depart into the highways and bring people to Him, to His wedding feast. We are to plant the seeds of the gospel of the kingdom of God in the uttermost parts of the earth (Acts 1:8). We understand, though, that we are solely in the seed-planting business. We are not in the growing business. That's the job of the Holy Spirit. And not all of the seeds that we plant will fall on fertile soil or will grow to maturity (Matthew 13:3–8). Hence, we see in Matthew 22:13 that some who come to the wedding will not be prepared to marry the king's son, and they will experience "weeping and gnashing of teeth."

When Scripture says in Matthew 28:19 to "go therefore and make disciples of all the nations," the Greek word here for *nations* is *ethnos*, which means "peoples" or "people groups." This is where we get the English word *ethnic*. So the translation in Matthew 28:19 for "nations" is not referring to geographical territories—it's referring to groups of people. So where are these people we are to depart to?

Steve Hickey frames the people groups as belonging to various spheres:

God wants the leaven of heaven to permeate the rest of the planet—the spheres of government, the spheres of media and the arts, the spheres of education, and the spheres of industry and the marketplace. God is not just interested in your local church.[1]

Similarly, C. Peter Wagner identifies various "molders of culture" that Christians can reach:

If the world is to be won, these are seven mountains that mold the culture and minds of men. Whoever controls these mountains controls the direction of the world and the harvest therein. The seven molders of culture are religion, family, government, arts and entertainment, media, business, and education, listed in random order, not in order of importance. Obviously each one of the seven can be subdivided many times.[2]

In the foreword to *The Legend of the Monk and the Merchant*, Dave Ramsey writes,

We should actively take possession of segments of the marketplace for Christ instead of surrendering them to the other side. We don't claim the church as God's turf and surrender the marketplace as Satan's. We're alive, active, and moving in both, and I believe God puts a call on our lives to redeem the business world for His glory. That's been the goal of my entire career.

Felipo and Alessio discover that they are *both* called to serve God—each in their own ways.

DISCUSSION

- Give some examples of how you can be in the highways and invite people to the wedding feast.

- What are some of the strategies and phrases you use to invite people to the wedding feast? (For example, "Can I pray for you and your health issue?")

- How do you deal with people who decline the invitation to the wedding feast?

- Are you currently clothed in a wedding garment, as talked about in Matthew 22:11? What is required of you to wear the wedding garment?

- In which of the seven mountains of our culture do you have a presence? How can you effectively plant the yeast of God into those mountains?

MONEY: GOOD OR EVIL?

C. Peter Wagner describes how money began to be seen as evil:

> Greek thinking... promoted the idea of the spiritual aspect of life as superior to the material aspect of life. The conclusion was that the more spiritual you are, the less material you will be. The monasteries and their monks adopted this philosophy and promoted it throughout the Middle Ages. Before long, all clergy, in order to attest their superior spirituality, were obligated to take vows of poverty. . . .
>
> Unfortunately, the vow of poverty has persisted in our churches.[1]

What does Scripture say about money? "For the love of money is a root of all kinds of evil, for which some have strayed from the faith in their greediness" (1 Timothy 6:10). Note that money itself is not a root of evil; "the love of money" is. It's an issue of the heart, of your attitude toward money. If you love anything and anyone more than God, you have, by definition, made that thing or person an idol. And God hates idolatry. He says: "You shall have no other gods before Me" (Exodus 20:3).

Money is amoral. It's your attitude toward it and what you do with it that God judges. Remember, it is God "who gives you power to get wealth" (Deuteronomy 8:18).

We see many wealthy people who were followers of Jesus: the Zebedees (who had servants [Mark 1:20]), Zacchaeus (a tax collector [Luke 19:2]), Matthew (another tax collector [Matthew 9:9]), the Roman centurion (Luke 7:2–8), Nicodemus ("a ruler of the Jews" [John 3:1]), and Joseph of Arimathea (Matthew 27:57), to name a few. And of course, the Old Testament is filled with God's people who had wealth: Abraham, Isaac, Jacob, Joseph, David, Solomon, and many others. So it is not wealth or lack of wealth that God judges— it is your heart's condition.

But we do understand from Scripture that there is the danger of "the deceitfulness of riches" (Mark 4:19).

Os Hillman, in his book *The Purposes of Money*[2], writes about four potholes on the road to prosperity:

1. Greed (1 Timothy 3:3)
2. Covetousness (Exodus 20:17; 1 Timothy 3:3)
3. Stinginess (Luke 6:29)
4. Self-reliance (Galatians 2:20)

He also talks about five common misconceptions concerning money:

1. My money is to buy anything I want.
2. My money measures my success.
3. Money is my security.
4. I can gain independence by having a lot of money.
5. Money defines my purpose in life.

First, in misconceptions one and two, *my money* is a misnomer. Jesus uses the parable of the talents to explain that God gives us stewardship over our lives: our money, time, and gifts (Matthew 25:14–30). All of these blessings are still His. He merely asks us to be productive with what He has left in our safekeeping.

Second, our success is measured by our service to others, not by money. Consider Jesus' words: "But he who is greatest among you shall be your servant" (Matthew 23:11). "But many who are first will be last, and the last first" (Matthew 19:30). In the wise words of an unknown person, "Financial success is merely a measurement of your service to others." As you offer people a service or product of value, the recipient is willing to pay you money proportionate to its value. This exchange is at the foundation of the free-market system.

Third, there is no security in earthly riches: "Do not lay up for yourselves treasures on earth, where moth and rust destroy and where thieves break in and steal; but lay up for yourselves treasures in heaven, where neither moth or rust destroys and where thieves do not break in and steal" (Matthew 6:19–20).

Finally, regarding misconceptions four and five, we understand that as Christians we are not seeking *independence*; we are committed to being *dependent* on Jesus as our Lord. We know what our purpose is as Christians: to love and serve Jesus with all that we have and are.

Romans 10:9 says that we will be saved if we confess Jesus as Lord. When we do so, we have committed to be His servants. In Philippians 1:1 Paul writes about how he and Timothy are "bondservants of Jesus Christ." A bondservant is one who freely gives up all his rights to serve his master and lord 100 percent.

In a similar vein, Galatians 2:20 says, "I have been crucified with Christ; it is no longer I who live, but Christ lives in me."

We read in Psalm 37:4, "Delight yourself also in the LORD, and He shall give you the desires of your heart." But my Jewish friends who are Hebrew scholars tell me that the Hebrew reads very different than this: "Delight yourself in the LORD, and you will fulfill the desires of His heart." In other words, if "your life is hidden with Christ" (Colossians 3:3), and if you no longer live (Galatians 2:20), then your desires are God's desires.

In John 5:19 Jesus said, "The Son can do nothing of Himself, but what He sees the Father do; for whatever He does, the Son also does in like manner." Like Jesus, we also are to "be imitators of God as dear children" (Ephesians 5:1).

We are to do nothing of ourselves, but only what we see the Father do.

DISCUSSION

- Reread pages 49–53, where Alessio has to deal with the priest's teaching on Luke 18:18–27. What did you understand these scriptures to be teaching?

- Have you or people you know believed that it is to your spiritual benefit to stay away from riches? Where does that attitude come from?

- Which of the four potholes on the road to prosperity have you had to deal with?

- What misconceptions have you had about making money?

Three Misconceptions That Are Deadly to the Advancement of the Kingdom of God

Misconception #1: It is the Responsibility of Others to Give Financial Support to My Ministry Activities.

Christians must follow the example of Paul, who was a tentmaker in the marketplace: "For you remember, brethren, our labor and toil; for laboring night and day, that we might not be a burden to any of you, we preached to you the gospel of God" (1 Thessalonians 2:9).

There has developed a flawed entitlement mentality within the body of believers. Rather than going to work to earn money for ministry activities, Christians have made the mailing of support letters an art form. It is *displaced responsibility* to the highest degree. The idea is to have another Christian toil and send money so that I don't have to work or give myself. Unfortunately, we ask our children to engage in this behavior as they seek support for short-term mission trips, teaching them laziness and entitlement at a very young age.

Certainly, there is nothing wrong with being in vocational ministry and being paid for your work: "Let the elders who rule well be counted worthy of double honor, especially those who labor in the word and doctrine. For the Scripture says, 'You shall not muzzle an ox while it treads out the grain,' and 'The laborer is worthy of his wages'" (1 Timothy 5:17–18). But these wages come from money tithed to the church fellowship. There is nothing in Scripture that teaches us to *beg* for financial support.

MISCONCEPTION #2: FINANCIAL BENEVOLENCE SHOULD BE EQUALLY SHOWN TO THOSE ABLE OR UNABLE TO WORK.

What does Scripture have to say about this idea? Paul warns, "If anyone will not work, neither shall he eat" (2 Thessalonians 3:10). And even more sternly: "If anyone does not provide for his own, and especially for those of his household, he has denied the faith and is worse than an unbeliever" (1 Timothy 5:8).

Imagine—worse than an unbeliever!

Here's what is true: Personal responsibility is commended and rewarded. Laziness and sloth are deadly sins (Proverbs 19:15). Recall Principle Three from Antonio's journal: "A MAN MUST DO WHATEVER HE CAN TO PROVIDE FOR HIS FAMILY."

MISCONCEPTION #3: WE SHOULD BE CONTENT WITH JUST ENOUGH MONEY TO MEET OUR BASIC NEEDS.

Let's again turn to Scripture to test this idea. Proverbs 13:22 indicates that it is selfish not to see past your own need: "A good man leaves an inheritance to his children's children."

In a sermon titled "The Use of Money," John Wesley preached a concept that can be summarized as, "Earn all you can, save all you can, give all you can."[1] That's prosperity with a purpose!

DISCUSSION

- How do you feel about giving financial support to individuals in ministry who can be raising the money themselves through their own work? (We are not talking about giving tithes.) How do you feel about asking individuals to financially support your ministry activities?

- How do you give money to the needy without enabling them and perpetuating the cycle of poverty?

- Are you moved to earn an income that goes beyond your personal financial needs? If yes, what do you do with financial abundance? If no, what is stopping you?

VOCATIONS AND VALUES

A ntonio travels with his grandson, Julio, to Rome. Antonio recognizes that their time together would change his grandson forever. Values about work, money, and character are passed from generation to generation and influence how we shape our lives.

"I had two fathers, a rich one and a poor one," Robert Kiyosaki writes in *Rich Dad, Poor Dad*, the best-selling business book ever written.[1] Note the differences in attitudes between the two men:

Poor Dad: Regularly said, "I can't afford it." [A statement that settles the matter]

Rich Dad: Asked himself, "How can I afford it?" [A question that forces us to think]

Poor Dad: Did not allow discussion of money or business at the dinner table.

Rich Dad: Encouraged discussion of money or business at the dinner table.

Poor Dad: Played it safe and did not take risks financially.
Rich Dad: Learned to manage financial risks.

Poor Dad: Believed a company or the government should take care of your needs.
Rich Dad: Believed in self-reliance and spoke out against the entitlement mentality.

Poor Dad: Taught his son how to write an impressive resume so he could find a good job.
Rich Dad: Taught his son to write strong business and financial plans so he could create jobs.[2]

We smile when we see a bumper sticker that reads, "I'm spending my children's inheritance." But remember that those who fall short in leaving an inheritance fall short in God's perfect plan: "A good man leaves an inheritance to his children's children, but the wealth of the sinner is stored up for the righteous" (Proverbs 13:22). Certainly, that would include a financial inheritance. Robert Kiyosaki writes, "It's not about income. It's about assets that continue to pay your family, even after you are gone."[3] For a good example, look no further than Antonio, who built a legacy business in Venetian trading beads that would continue to generate income for many generations.

To ensure that there will be a financial inheritance, it's important to engage in estate planning and prepare a will so that your money goes to your heirs and not to the government. It's also important that you have insurance so that your assets are not consumed by a health emergency or by an accident involving your car or house.

However, inheritances aren't limited to money. Each of us inherits, and will in turn pass on, values that shape every aspect of our lives, including our families, our faith, and our finances. Like Kiyosaki, we must be intentional about sorting through the values we have inherited, figuring out which ones to keep and which to discard. We also need to be purposeful about choosing which values to pass on to future generations.

Dave Ramsey advocates teaching children money principles while they are still very small. Some of his beliefs:

- "Teach kids about money as young as preschool age and no later than third grade."[4]

- "Start paying [your children] a commission for chores they do around the house."[5]

- "Do not give [children] an allowance. . . . Send them off to work. Child abuse is letting a kid sit in front of a

TV all day playing video games and eating junk food. Kids need to understand what a little dirt under the fingernails means. Delivering newspapers, mowing lawns, or working at a concession stand are some appropriate jobs they can handle."[6]

Who we learn from—the company we keep—is just as important as what we learn. At fourteen, Julio was placed under special tutelage to prepare him for the family business. Similarly, Antonio had a lot to learn from his mentor, Alessio.

Even if you can't spend a day with a successful person, you can sit at his or her feet through CD and DVD recordings and through books. But choose your mentor carefully; as 1 Corinthians 15:33 warns, "Do not be misled: 'Bad company corrupts good character'" (NIV).

A mentor can help you clarify your calling. It was clear from his youth that Antonio had an entrepreneurial anointing: he "loved to work . . . and think," and he was often "developing ideas," pioneering new methods, and seeking out "innovations." It wasn't until his apprenticeship with Alessio, however, that Antonio became certain of his vocation.

A vocation is more than a job. It's your calling. "When you do it, it's not really *work* at all," Antonio tells Julio. "When a person discovers his vocation, he does it gladly and with joy."

Antonio's father, Felipo, found his own calling in the church: "For him, it was where he felt most alive. And that's what happens when you discover your true vocation."

DISCUSSION

- What values were passed to you from your previous generations? What are you exposing your children to that will change them forever?

- Poverty mind-sets are passed on from generation to generation. What baggage have you inherited, and how are you ensuring your children that this baggage is not passed onto them?

- Do you ever take your children to great places and talk to them about how these places came to be?

- Have you done estate planning? Do you have a will? Do you have insurance to protect your assets?

- Who are the people who influence you? Who are some of the people you'd love to hang out with for a day?

- What is a calling? Who gets called? How do you know what your calling is?

- What do you love to do? What are you passionate about? What makes you feel most alive?

- Why are so many people frustrated and unfulfilled in their jobs today? How would you advise a person who is unhappy in her job?

Frugality, Diligence, and Divine Innovations

lessio was immeasurably influential and wealthy, but Antonio "was amazed at the simple way this successful merchant lived and yet maintained one of the greatest business empires in the world." Antonio "was determined to learn from him."

Dave Ramsey advocates living a simple lifestyle, regardless of your income. Alessio's decision not to live extravagantly reflects the wisdom that Ramsey repeatedly shares on his daily radio programs, such as "Live like no one else so you can live like no one else" and "Act your wage."[1] Alessio avoids falling into the common trap that Ramsey warns against: "We buy things we don't need with money we don't have to impress people we don't like."[2] A good example of this is Ramsey's exhortation to purchase pre-owned cars instead of new ones. "I'm not against having new cars," he says. "I'm against them having you. We spend a tremendous amount impressing somebody at the stoplight who we'll never meet. It makes you broke and it keeps you broke."[3] Similarly, Robert Kiyosaki, author of *Rich Dad, Poor Dad*, explains the importance of limiting your purchase of depreciating assets.

But unfortunately, Alessio's decision is a rare one. In *WEIRD: Because Normal Isn't Working*, Craig Groeschel writes, "Being weird is a virtue and… 'normal' in today's culture is broke. Finances: normal is debt, worry, tension, fear. Normal is broke. Credit card debt? Normal. Paying only minimums? Normal."[4]

Scripture has plenty to say on the value of living simply and frugally:

There is desirable treasure, and oil in the dwelling of the wise, but a foolish man squanders it. (Proverbs 21:20)

I have learned to be content whatever the circumstances. I know what it is to be in need, and I know what it is to have plenty. I have learned the secret of being content in any and every situation, whether well fed or hungry, whether living in plenty or in want. (Philippians 4:11–12 NIV)

Keep your lives free from the love of money and be content with what you have, because God has said, "Never will I leave you; never will I forsake you." (Hebrews 13:5 NIV)

Make it your ambition to lead a quiet life: You should mind

your own business and work . . . so that your daily life may win the respect of outsiders and so that you will not be dependent on anybody. (1 Thessalonians 4:11–12 NIV)

"Do not lay up for yourselves treasures on earth, where moth and rust destroy and where thieves break in and steal; but lay up for yourselves treasures in heaven, where neither moth nor rust destroys and where thieves do not break in and steal. For where your treasure is, there your heart will be also." (Matthew 6:19–21)

The call to a simple lifestyle was even codified at the 1974 International Congress on World Evangelization: "All of us are shocked by the poverty of millions and disturbed by the injustices which cause it. Those of us who live in affluent circumstances accept our duty to develop a simple life-style in order to contribute more generously to both relief and evangelism."[5]

Diligence and determination are the keys to building wealth that lasts. Remember Principle One from Antonio's journal: "WORK HARD AND GOD WILL PROSPER YOU," which is supported by Deuteronomy 28:8: "The LORD will send a blessing on your barns and on everything *you put your hand to*" (NIV, emphasis added).

So does hard work always pay off? Yes and no, according to Robert Kiyosaki:

"If you work really hard, you'll be okay." What a pile of

baloney! And what's so tragic about it is that most people have been brainwashed to believe it, and they do believe it, even though we're all surrounded by tons of evidence to the contrary. What evidence? Just look around you. Do you know anyone who has worked really hard his entire life, only to end up living a life that hovers just above—or just below—the indignity and heartbreak called "subsistence level?" . . .

The world is full of people who work hard and are most definitely not okay. . . . The problem is that the hard-work myth is just that: a myth. . . . I'm not saying that building wealth and financial freedom does not take hard work; it does, and lots of it. . . . Working hard at making money will never create wealth. People who work for income work harder and harder, only to be taxed more and more. Forget working hard at making money: all you'll do is spend it, and then you have to work hard all over again.[6]

So how can one build wealth? Antonio's story suggests that disruptive innovations may be key. A disruptive innovation or technology is an innovation that helps create a new market and value network and eventually goes on to disrupt an existing market and value network, displacing an earlier technology. Although the invention of the automobile was transformational, it was not a disruptive innovation because early automobiles were expensive luxury items that did not disrupt the market for horse-drawn vehicles. It was not until the invention of the assembly line by Ford, which caused automobiles to be produced more quickly and become more affordable, that the automobile became a disruptive innovation. Now the phrase *buggy-whip maker* has become a popular description of business models that are destroyed by disruptive technologies.

Antonio's creation of Venetian trade beads and his success in persuading the business world of his idea to use these as a universal currency are good examples of disruptive innovations.

Ask the Holy Spirit to inspire you with creative ideas, with disruptive innovations. Success in the marketplace is finding a need and filling it.

DISCUSSION

- If it's true that we learn more from what people *do* than from what they *say*, what was the lesson that Antonio learned from Alessio's simple lifestyle?

- Reread Ramsey's principles presented at the beginning of the lesson. What is Ramsey saying?

- Some people make millions, spend millions, and in the end are broke. Why?

- What needs have you identified in the marketplace? Can you innovate, through the help of the Holy Spirit, solutions to those needs?

LAZY MEN AND
LAZY MONEY

Even though Antonio's trading beads succeeded relatively quickly—"within three years, the beads were standard in Venice"—Antonio still faced challenges. "The past years had not been easy," he tells Julio. Getting rich quick is not God's usual way.

People often want wealth handed to them. Many times Christians are in this group. We think that praying is a substitute for putting our hands to the plow. God's teaching in Scripture repeatedly explains the laws of sowing and reaping. The size of the harvest is in direct proportion to the measure that was sown and the price that was paid.

Dave Ramsey teaches a Momentum Theorem: focused intensity (hard, hard work), over time, multiplied by a great big God, is the equation for increase and momentum.[1] If any of the three factors in the equation is missing, the increase is not exponential.

Most today are shackled wage slaves for whom working *harder* won't increase incomes. Wisdom tells us to work *smarter*.

Jesus teaches about "lazy money" in Matthew 25:14–30, the parable of the talents. Lazy money is money that is not working for you, money that is just sitting there. Where can we find extra money that can work for us?

- Cancel your subscriptions, your gym membership, or your cable.

- Actively manage your money to eliminate late fees, finance charges, interest, and ATM fees.

- Avoid unnecessary purchases or payments, and think twice about taking on new responsibilities, such as caring for a pet.

- Eat all your groceries (we throw away 25 percent of the food we buy).[2]

- Dine in.

- Bundle services.

- Ask for discounts, deals, and lower rates.

- Buy fewer Christmas presents.

- Get rid of expensive habits or hobbies.

The truth is that God has bigger dreams for us than we do: "'For I know the plans I have for you,' declares the LORD, 'plans to proper you and not to harm you, plans to give you hope and a future'" (Jeremiah 29:11 NIV). God "is able to do exceedingly abundantly above all that we ask or think, according to the power that works in us" (Ephesians 3:20). Sadly, we end up shrinking our dreams to match our incomes, instead of increasing our incomes to match our God-given dreams.

Small thinking is not God's will or way. Large thinking often requires large incomes, but large incomes don't just happen. They are a product of "Rich Dad" thinking, of Dave Ramsey thinking, of hard work, time, and prayer. And recall Principle Two from Antonio's journal: "FINANCIAL PROSPERITY IS OFTEN CONNECTED TO SOUL PROSPERITY." Alessio reminds Antonio of 3 John 2: "Beloved, I pray that you may prosper in all things and be in health, just as your soul propsers." God wants us to succeed, which we can do only when we are in relationship with Him.

Habakkuk 2:2–3 offers encouragement for the journey: "Write the vision and make it plain on tablets, that he may run who reads it. For the vision is yet for an appointed time; but at the end it will speak, and it will not lie. Though it tarries, wait for it; because it will surely come, it will not tarry."

Finally, it is important to recognize that God expects more from those entrusted with more: "From everyone who has been given much, much will be demanded; and from the one who has been entrusted with much, much more will be asked" (Luke 12:48 NIV).

DISCUSSION

- What does "hard work" mean to you? What price are you willing to pay to become financially free?

- How can you work smarter?

- How can you make lazy money work for you?

- What does soul prosperity mean to you?

- If God is no respecter of persons and treats us all the same, why does He expect more from the wealthy?

- Reread Luke 12:48. Could "much is given" be referring to more than money? Could that phrase be talking about time and talent also? If yes, then is it possible that poor people will be judged according to the potential God gave them?

ADVERSITY AND
ADVANCEMENT

In *A View from the Zoo*, Gary Richmond describes the birth of a giraffe:

The first thing to emerge are the baby giraffe's front hooves and head. A few minutes later the pluck newborn calf is hurled forth, falls ten feet, and lands on its back. Within seconds, he rolls to an upright position with his legs tucked under his body. From this position he considers the world for the first time and shakes off the last vestiges of the birthing fluid from his ears and eyes.

The mother giraffe lowers her head long enough to take a quick look. Then she positions herself directly over her calf. She waits for a minute and then she does the most unreasonable thing. She swings her long pendulous leg outward and kicks her baby, so that it is sent sprawling head over heels.

When it doesn't get up, the violent process is repeated over and over again. The struggle to rise is momentous. As the baby giraffe grows tired, the mother kicks it again to stimulate its efforts. . . . Finally the calf stands for the first time on wobbly legs. Then the mother giraffe does the most remarkable thing. She kicks it off its feet again. Why? She wants it to remember how it got up. In the world, baby giraffes must be able to get up as quickly as possible in order to stay with the herd, where there is safety. Lions, hyenas, leopards, and wild hunting dogs all enjoy young giraffes, and they'd get it too, if the mother didn't teach her calf to get up quickly and get with it.[1]

In this session we will see how God is like that mama giraffe as He uses trials to knock us down so we can get back up again, better and stronger.

After Antonio watches his factory burn to the ground, Alessio discusses Principle Four: "TRIALS DEVELOP YOUR CHARACTER, PREPARING YOU FOR INCREASED BLESSINGS." This principle is grounded in Romans 5:3–4: "We also glory in tribulations, knowing that tribulation produces perseverance; and perseverance, character; and character, hope."

It is a myth that successful people don't have the struggles that you and I do and that successful companies experience only minor setbacks.

In their book *Built to Last: Successful Habits of Visionary Companies*, Jim Collins and Jerry Porras write of many companies that went through their share of struggles:

Walt Disney faced a serious cash flow crisis in 1939 which forced it to go public; later, in the early 1980s, the company nearly ceased to exist as an independent entity as corporate raiders eyed its depressed stock price. Boeing had serious difficulties in the mid-1930s, the late 1940s, and again in the early 1970s when it laid off over sixty thousand employees. 3M began life as a failed mine and almost went out of business in the early 1900s. Hewlett-Packard faced severe cutbacks in 1945; in 1990, it watched its stock drop to a price below book value. Sony had repeated product failures during its first five years of life (1945–1950), and in the 1970s saw its Beta format lose to VHS in the battle for market dominance in VCRs. Ford posted one of the largest annual losses in American business history ($3.3 billion in three years) in the early 1980s before it began an impressive turnaround and long-needed revitalization. Citicorp (founded in 1812, the same year Napoleon marched to Moscow) languished in the late 1800s, during the 1930s depression, and again in the late 1980s when it struggled with its global loan portfolio. IBM was nearly bankrupt in 1914, then again in 1921, and [was] having trouble again in the early 1990s.[2]

Sometimes the problems we face are of our own making. Alessio gently points out to Antonio his error in constructing too many furnaces under one roof. When faced with such mistakes, we might be reluctant to admit our part in the situation. But Antonio models how to adhere to Principle Five: "TAKE RESPONSIBILITY FOR PROBLEMS THAT ARE A RESULT OF YOUR OWN BAD DECISIONS. DON'T DISPLACE BLAME."

Finally, Alessio encourages Antonio with Principle Six: "SEE CHALLENGES AS STEPPING STONES, NOT AS OBSTACLES." It's easy to wallow in despair, to feel like our circumstances are insurmountable. But Alessio helps Antonio see that the loss of the factory can actually accelerate the growth of Antonio's business. Much like the mother giraffe's kicks are necessary steps for the baby's survival, challenges are necessary for the growth of any endeavor.

There is a story of a young boy who came upon a cocoon that had a caterpillar in it. He had been taught that the caterpillar was turning into a butterfly and would then struggle to break out of the cocoon so it could fly. Being bighearted, the boy pulled out his penknife and made a slit in the cocoon to save the butterfly from the pain of getting free. He didn't understand that it was the struggle of breaking out of the cocoon that strengthened the butterfly's wings and would allow him to fly.

Many times we act like the young boy and try to save people from struggling, not understanding that God has told us that it's the struggle that develops character and allows us to survive life.

When the challenges seem overwhelming, remember the

advice found in 1 Peter 5:7: "Throw all your anxiety onto [Jesus], because he cares about you" (CEB). We are reminded, "Cast your burden on the Lord—he will support you!" (Psalm 55:22 CEB). When we trust God with our worries, we find ourselves in a much better position to tackle whatever comes our way. After all, "If God is for us, who can be against us?" (Romans 8:31).

Discussion

- What have been your biggest vocational setbacks, losses, or disappointments? Share a time when discouragement nearly derailed you from your dreams. What were the lessons you learned from your hard times?

- If fire swept through your vocational life right now, would you be mad or thankful? If you are already in the middle of the fire, what do you think it will take for you to grow past the challenges you are currently facing?

- What would you say to a friend who said to you what Antonio said to Alessio: "Well, it's obvious that God is closing a door in my business. Why else would He allow my factory to be burned?"

- What would you say to a person who turned down

a promotion because he didn't want the increased challenges that came with it?

- Do you ever see Christians displace responsibility, blaming Satan when it is their own bad decisions that have caused their challenges? How do we know if adversity is of the devil?

- Why is personal responsibility increasingly rare today? List excuses that you've seen people use for their failures in the workplace.

- Are you carrying your burdens, or are you letting the Lord carry them?

BOLDNESS IN BUSINESS: OVERCOMING FEAR AND INTIMIDATION

Antonio does indeed recover from the fire that burned down the bead factory. Just when his business has returned to successful levels, Antonio finds himself on a journey to meet with Ahmad, the feared merchant-pirate.

What does *FEAR* stand for?

1. False Evidence Appearing Real
2. Finding Excuses And Reasons
3. Failure Expected And Received
4. Forget Everything And Run

Fear is temporary. Regret is forever. Action gets rid of fear.

Let's look at one of the most feared villains in the Bible. Goliath was big and scary. He strutted around for forty days, shouting out his proclamations and terrifying Israel: "As [David] was talking with them, Goliath, the Philistine champion from Gath, stepped out from his lines and shouted his usual defiance, and David heard it. Whenever the Israelites saw the man, they all fled from him in great fear" (1 Samuel 17:23–24 NIV).

David ran too! But eventually he came back and strutted boldly up to the giant. What changed? David replaced his fears with truth.

Ahmad, the merchant-pirate, was legendary in his ferociousness. But in reality, Antonio discovers, "he was not a fierce man at all, but rather one who was smart and articulate." Antonio would never have discovered the truth about Ahmad had he been unwilling to face his fear.

The Bible is clear that fear is not God's way. Second Timothy 1:7 says, "For God has not given us a spirit of fear, but of power and of love and of a sound mind." The word for "sound mind" in the Greek is *sophronismos*, which means "controlled, disciplined thought." So fear does not come from God; it is a spirit that comes from the enemy. Controlled, disciplined thought comes from God, and God expects us to bring "every thought into captivity" (2 Corinthians 10:5). We are to "be anxious for nothing" (Philippians 4:6). Jesus Himself tells us, "Do not worry about your life" (Matthew 6:25).

Antonio shares with Alessio his anxiety about meeting with Ahmad, but Alessio responds with Principle Seven: "BE meek before god but bold before men." Meekness is not timidity and cowering in fear.

Matthew 5:5 shows that God has a special heart for the meek: "Blessed are the meek, for they shall inherit the earth." The Bible closely associates meekness with two people, neither of which was lacking boldness: Moses and Jesus.

Numbers 12:3 tells us that "Moses was very meek, above all the men which were upon the face of the earth" (kjv). Yet once Moses jumped into the middle of a fight to defend a slave. Later, Moses stood up against the most powerful ruler on earth, Pharaoh.

Matthew 11:29 tells us that "[Jesus was] meek and lowly in heart" (kjv). Yet Jesus went into the temple and turned over the tables of the money changers, and they fled from the premises. Jesus on many occasions strongly criticized the Jewish rulers, the Pharisees.

Moses and Jesus both showed healthy aggression that allowed them to fulfill their purposes. In business, healthy aggression is an intense desire to fill a need, to serve and excel more than others in that service. Charles E. Phillips Jr., former CEO of Oracle Corporation, the world's largest enterprise software company, remarks that aggressiveness has its place: "Aggressiveness is not a bad thing; companies that are not too aggressive in this industry tend to end up as being part of an aggressive company," he says.[1] In Phillips's view, aggression should motivate people to excel, driving them to win customers and solve problems:

I love to compete. I love the game. I love to win. And that's what I use internally to motivate people. Rallying people around you on a mission and focusing on the outside world and not fighting each other. . . . That is what makes the place (Oracle) fun. I would not want to be at a company that did not feel it has any energy or assertiveness.[2]

God wants His people to be shrewd in the marketplace. *Shrewd* means "marked by sound judgment and practical intelligence; inclined to use cunning"; synonyms include "astute, sharp, keen, sagacious, clever, cunning, crafty, calculating, tricky, sly, [and] cagey."[3]

"The master commended the dishonest manager because he had acted shrewdly. For the people of this world are more shrewd in dealing with their own kind than are the people of the light. I tell you, use worldly wealth to gain friends for yourselves, so that when it is gone, you will be welcomed into eternal dwellings." (Luke 16:8–9 NIV)

"Behold, I send you out as sheep in the midst of wolves. Therefore, be as wise as serpents and harmless as doves." (Matthew 10:16)

We are to walk in love and humility, humility being the knowledge that all you are and all you have is by the grace of God. But we are to be as "wise as serpents" while dealing in the world and in business, asking God for wisdom and discernment and divine strategies to aggressively take dominion in the marketplace.

DISCUSSION

• In what ways do people feed fears that paralyze them vocationally? What happens to people who aren't assertive or aggressive in their vocations?

• If you were to take a risk in your vocation, what would you gain? What frightens you about taking that risk? What's the worst thing that could happen if it turned out badly? If the worst thing happened, what would you do? What could you do to minimize this possibility?

• In terms of vocational assertiveness, which term defines you best?

1. *Prospector*—actively seeking to expand into new markets and stimulate opportunities
2. *Defender*—maintaining a secure and relatively stable environment
3. *Analyzer*—watching closely the developments in the industry, but not acting until you are certain the timing is right

4. *Reactor*—reacting to events as they occur instead of having a proactive strategy

- How do you respond to those who think Christianity produces spineless, timid, powerless pushovers?

- Why would the monks tell Alessio that being aggressive in business is a mistake?

- Should Christians be aggressive in business? Why or why not? What are the limits and boundaries we, as Christians, should put on aggressiveness in business?

Budgeting, Borrowing, and Lending

Alessio teaches Antonio several principles regarding the smart handling of money.

Principle Eight, "LIVE DEBT-FREE AND BELOW YOUR MEANS," finds its biblical basis in Romans 13:8: "Let no debt remain outstanding, except the continuing debt to love one another" (NIV). Unfortunately, debt has become an acceptable burden to carry in our society. When the Forbes 400 were asked, "What is the most important key to building wealth?" 75 percent said it was living and staying debt-free.[1] Yet 60 percent of Americans do not pay off the monthly balance on their credit cards.[2] Dave Ramsey observes, "Debt has been marketed to us in so many forms so aggressively since the 1960's that to even imagine living without it requires a complete paradigm shift."[3]

Many Americans fail to keep Principle Eight in mind when faced with how to pay for a car. Although leasing may seem like an attractive option, it's actually the most expensive way to operate a vehicle.[4] The most financially responsible way to purchase a car is by paying the full amount in cash.

Principle Nine is the key to debt-free living: "ALWAYS KEEP TO YOUR BUDGET." Money flows *from* those who don't know how to manage it *to* those who know how to manage it. Either you will learn to manage money, or it will manage you! Managed money goes further. By tracking your expenses and earnings and working from a plan, you can avoid spontaneous, panicked, or out-of-control spending. Make a plan for building wealth—and stick to it!

Principle Ten, "LOANING MONEY DESTROYS RELATION-SHIPS," is backed by several Bible verses from Proverbs:

> He who puts up security for another will surely suffer. (Proverbs 11:15 NIV 1984)

> It's stupid to guarantee someone else's loan. (Proverbs 17:18 CEV)

> Do not be among those who give pledges, among those who become guarantors for debts. If you have nothing with which to pay, why should he take your bed from under you? (Proverbs 22:26–27 NASB)

When and if someone you have loaned money to can't pay you back, you now have a strained relationship. If you are moved to give people financial help, then *give* it to them.

Don't *lend* it to them. (We will discuss the importance of healthy giving in session 12.)

In their book *When Helping Hurts: How to Alleviate Poverty Without Hurting the Poor and Yourself*, authors Steve Corbett and Brian Fikkert write:

> Many observers, including [the two of us], believe that when North American Christians *do* attempt to alleviate poverty, the methods used often do considerable harm to both the materially poor and the materially non-poor. Our concern is not just that these methods are wasting human, spiritual, financial, and organizational resources, but that these methods are actually exacerbating the very problems they are trying to solve.[5]

Christians are to help those who *can't* help themselves, not enable those who *can* help themselves.

Discussion

- Why is it such a challenge to live debt-free?

- Have you done a cash-flow analysis, determining how much extra money you have each month, or how short you are on your cash-flow each month? If you have a negative cash-flow, what can you do or should you do to remedy that situation?

- Have you set boundaries on what you spend on clothing, food, and so on? In other words, do you have a budget for how much you will spend each month in different areas of your life? Does this budget include line items for things such as eating out, entertainment, and coffee runs?

- Do you have a savings plan? A strategy for building a retirement fund?

- How do you determine if giving someone money is helping him or hurting/enabling him?

Mentorship and Partnering

Alessio mentored Antonio for many years. It was through this relationship that Antonio gained the wisdom that allowed him to make a difference in the world.

We touched briefly on the importance of mentoring in Session Five. Proverbs stresses the importance of learning from those who have gone before: "Where there is no counsel, the people fall; but in the multitude of counselors there is safety" (Proverbs 11:14). Proverbs 13:20 reiterates, "He who walks with wise men will be wise."

Enter into a mentor-mentee relationship with a clear sense of purpose. In his book *Mentor Like Jesus*, Regi Campbell writes,

Mentoring is not about *coming to know* something; that would be education. Mentoring is not about learning *to do* something; that would be training.

Mentoring is about showing someone *how to be something.*[1]

Focus on the Family identifies a number of factors to consider when choosing a mentor: honesty, openness and transparency, a commitment to the relationship, and success in the areas of life that are important to you. A mentor should be comfortable not only with teaching you but also with learning from you. Your agenda, not your mentor's, should drive your conversations. The ideal mentor believes in your ability to succeed, and he or she helps you define your dream and what needs to be done to achieve it.[2] If the list of qualifications seems overwhelming, remember that "the simple truth is that what you're really looking for is a person who you know cares for you, believes in you, and encourages you."[3]

The Holy Spirit reveals all truth (John 16:13). So while you should trust your mentor, you should never follow him or her blindly. Test your mentor's advice against Scripture, and don't be afraid to ask questions if something troubles you.

We typically think of mentoring as a one-way, hierarchal relationship. But as Antonio sought counsel from Alessio, the two men were in reality partnering with each other.

God is a God of relationships. Above all, He wants a relationship with us. Recall how God searched for Adam and Eve in the garden: "Then the LORD God called to Adam and said to him, 'Where are you?'"(Genesis 3:9). It was Adam and Eve who were hiding from God, not the reverse: "Adam and his wife hid themselves from the presence of the LORD God among the trees of the garden" (Genesis 3:8).

In Genesis 1:26, Scripture explains that we are made according to God's likeness. We have His nature. We are relational beings because He is relational. And God desires partnership with us. He could have parted the Red Sea on His own, but He said to Moses, "Lift up your rod, and stretch out your hand over the sea and divide it" (Exodus 14:16). God chooses to work with and through people to get things done on planet Earth.

He also desires that we work in partnership with each other. This is why Principle Twelve states, "UNDERSTAND THE POWER OF PARTNERSHIP."

Let's look at what the Bible has to say about co-laboring together for God's purpose:

We are God's fellow workers. (1 Corinthians 3:9)

"For in this the saying is true: 'One sows and another reaps.'" (John 4:37)

For in fact the body is not one member but many. If the foot should say, "Because I am not a hand, I am not of the body," is it therefore not of the body? . . . Now indeed there are many members, yet one body. (1 Corinthians 12:14–15, 20)

We need each other in order to be fully functional. In partnership, we can do so much more than we can do individually.

DISCUSSION

- Do you have mentors in your life? If so, who are they?

- How do you decide who to choose as a mentor?

- All of us need a mentor, but all of us are also called to be mentors. The Bible calls it *being discipled* and *being called to disciple*. Whom have you chosen to disciple or mentor?

- Whom are you partnering with for the advancement of the kingdom of God?

- What are the dynamics of *your* partnership with God?

A LIFE OF GIVING IS A LIFE WORTH LIVING

Principle Eleven, "SET ASIDE THE FIRST 10 PERCENT TO HONOR GOD," points to the importance of tithing. Tithing is giving 10 percent of your taxable income to the storehouse, the spiritual place where you are fed. Malachi 3:8–10 illustrates how strongly God feels about tithing:

> "Will a mere mortal rob God? Yet you rob me.
>
> "But you ask, 'How are we robbing you?'
>
> "In tithes and offerings. You are under a curse—your whole nation—because you are robbing me. Bring the whole tithe into the storehouse, that there may be food in my house. Test me in this," says the LORD Almighty, "and see if I will not throw open the floodgates of heaven and pour out so much blessing that there will not be room enough to store it." (NIV)

Offerings are gifts you give outside of your tithe. God desires both tithes and offerings.

Blessed people bless people. Being blessed, we are to bless others. As stewards, God's overseers of His resources, we are to be conduits through which money, time, and talent flow.

We see God's heart for the hurting, wounded, and needy throughout the Bible. According to Ephesians 5:1, we are to "be imitators of God as dear children." As imitators, we should have the same giving hearts. Richard Stearns, the current president of World Vision U.S., writes in his book *The Hole in Our Gospel* about the prayer of Bob Pierce, World Vision's founder: "'Let my heart be broken by the things that break the heart of God.'"[1]

Consider just a few of the biblical commands to care for the less fortunate by sharing our wealth of resources:

"For the poor will never cease from the land; therefore I command you, saying, 'You shall open your hand wide to your brother, to your poor and your needy, in your land.'" (Deuteronomy 15:11)

Defend the poor and fatherless; do justice to the afflicted and needy. Deliver the poor and needy; free them from the hand of the wicked. (Psalm 82:3–4)

"'Come, you blessed of My Father, inherit the kingdom prepared for you from the foundation of the world: for I was hungry and you gave Me food; I was thirsty and you gave Me drink; I was a stranger and you took Me in; I was naked and you clothed Me; I was sick and you visited Me; I was in prison and you came to Me.'

"Then the righteous will answer Him, saying, 'Lord, when did we see You hungry and feed You, or thirsty and give You drink? When did we see You a stranger and take You in, or naked and clothe You? Or when did we see You sick, or in prison, and come to You?' And the King will answer and say to them, 'Assuredly, I say to you, inasmuch as you did it to one of the least of these My brethren, you did it to Me.'" (Matthew 25:34–40)

Let us not forget, either, the way that giving blesses the giver. Martyred missionary Jim Elliot recognized this concept when he stated, "He is no fool who gives what he cannot keep to gain what he cannot lose."[2]

We hold on to our riches at the risk of great peril. The prophet Ezekiel wrote that Sodom's cardinal sin was wealth-induced arrogance and lack of concern for the poor, not the sexual immorality that we more commonly associate with its violent destruction: "Now this was the sin of your sister Sodom: She and her daughters were arrogant, overfed and unconcerned; they did not help the poor and needy" (Ezekiel 16:49 NIV).

DISCUSSION

• Have you committed to tithing? If not, what is holding you back?

• Recall John 15:12–13: "This is My commandment, that you love one another as I have loved you. Greater love has no one than this, than to lay down one's life for his friends." During Jesus' time on earth, He laid down His life for those He was with, freely giving of His money, time, and gifts. Then, in His love for us, Jesus physically laid down His life and died for us. In what ways are you laying down your money, time, and gifts for people, displaying the love for one another that Jesus commands of us?

• Matthew 25 speaks of ministering to the needs of the hungry, the poor, the foreigner, the sick, and the imprisoned. Do you feel pulled to work with any of these specific groups? What small action can you take today to address the needs of God's hurting people?

NOTES

SESSION ONE: THE INACCURATE DIVISION BETWEEN THE
MONK AND THE MERCHANT, BETWEEN CLERGY AND LAITY
1. Robert Fraser, *Marketplace Christianity: Discovering the Kingdom
   Purpose of the Marketplace*, 2nd ed. (Overland Park, KS: New Grid
   Publishing, 2006), 7–8.
2. C. H. (Charles) Spurgeon, *Lectures to My Students* (Grand Rapids:
   Zondervan, 1954), 22.

SESSION TWO: CALLED TO OPERATE PRIMARILY OUTSIDE THE
MEETING PLACE
1. Steve Hickey, *Momentum: God's Ever-Increasing Kingdom* (Lake
   Mary, FL: Creation House, 2009), 26.
2. C. Peter Wagner, *Dominion! How Kingdom Action Can Change the
   World* (Grand Rapids: Chosen Books, 2008), 144.

SESSION THREE: MONEY: GOOD OR EVIL?
1. C. Peter Wagner, *The Church in the Workplace: How God's People
   Can Transform Society* (Ventura, CA: Regal Books, 2006), 56–57.
2. Os Hillman, *The Purposes of Money* (Alpharetta, GA: Aslan Group
   Publishing, 2000).

SESSION FOUR: THREE MISCONCEPTIONS THAT ARE DEADLY TO
THE ADVANCEMENT OF THE KINGDOM OF GOD
1. John Wesley, "The Use of Money," sermon, *Sermons on Several*

Occasions, 1771. Wesley's philosophy, as it appears in the text from the 1872 edition, edited by Thomas Jackson, is "Having, First, gained all you can, and Secondly saved all you can, Then 'give all you can.'" See the full text of the sermon at http://www.umcmission .org/Find-Resources/Global-Worship-and-Spiritual-Growth/John -Wesley-Sermons/Sermon-50-The-Use-of-Money.

SESSION FIVE: VOCATIONS AND VALUES

1. Robert T. Kiyosaki, *Rich Dad, Poor Dad: What the Rich Teach Their Kids About Money—That the Poor and the Middle Class Do Not!* (New York: Warner Books, 1997), 15, 16.
2. Ibid. The comparisons between the Poor Dad and the Rich Dad are paraphrased.
3. Robert T. Kiyosaki, *The Business of the 21st Century* (Lake Dallas, TX: Dreambuilders, 2010), 39.
4. "Top 3 Kids & Money Q&A," Dave Ramsey website, http:// www.daveramsey.com/article/top-3-kids-and-money-qa /lifeandmoney_kidsandmoney/.
5. Ibid.
6. Ibid.

SESSION SIX: FRUGALITY, DILIGENCE, AND DIVINE INNOVATIONS

1. Listen to Dave Ramsey's radio show at http://www.daveramsey .com/radio/home/#listenlive-tab.
2. Dave Ramsey, *The Total Money Makeover: A Proven Plan for Financial Fitness*, 3rd ed. (Nashville: Thomas Nelson, 2009), 30.
3. Ramsey, http://thinkexist.com/quotation/i-m-not-against-people -having-new-cars-i-m/432490.html.
4. Craig Groeschel, *WEIRD: Because Normal Isn't Working* (Grand Rapids: Zondervan, 2011), 18.
5. International Congress on World Evangelization, "The Lausanne Covenant," Lausanne, Switzerland, 1974, http://www.lausanne

.org/en/gatherings/issue-based2/easneye-1986.html?id=26.

6. Robert T. Kiyosaki, *The Business of the 21st Century* (Lake Dallas, TX: Dreambuilders, 2010), 28.

SESSION SEVEN: LAZY MEN AND LAZY MONEY

1. "Building Unstoppable Momentum," Dave Ramsey website, http://www.daveramsey.com/article/building-unstoppable-momentum/lifeandmoney_church/.

2. Tara Parker-Pope, "From Farm to Fridge to Garbage Can," *New York Times*, November 1, 2010, http://well.blogs.nytimes.com/2010/11/01/from-farm-to-fridge-to-garbage-can/. The article cites Jonathan Bloom, author of *American Wasteland: How America Throws Away Nearly Half Its Food*, who "estimates that as much as 25 percent of the food we bring into our homes is wasted."

SESSION EIGHT: ADVERSITY AND ADVANCEMENT

1. Excerpt from Gary Richmond's *A View from the Zoo* quoted in Roy B. Zuck, *The Speaker's Quote Book: Over 5,000 Illustrations and Quotations for All Occasions, Revised and Expanded* (Grand Rapids: Kregel Publications, 2009), 514.

2. Jim Collins and Jerry I. Porras, *Built to Last: Successful Habits of Visionary Companies* (New York: HarperCollins, 1997), 3–4.

SESSION NINE: BOLDNESS IN BUSINESS: OVERCOMING FEAR AND INTIMIDATION

1. Charles E. Phillips Jr., quoted in Gita Piramal, "Want to Succeed? Be Aggressive!" March 3, 2005, http://www.rediff.com/money/2005/mar/03spec.htm.

2. Ibid.

3. http://vocabulary-vocabulary.com/dictionary/shrewd.php.

SESSION TEN: BUDGETING, BORROWING, AND LENDING

1. Dave Ramsey, *The Total Money Makeover: A Proven Plan for*

Financial Fitness, 3rd ed. (Nashville: Thomas Nelson, 2009), 23.

2. Ibid., 41.

3. Dave Ramsey, *Financial Peace University: 91 Days to Beat Debt . . . and Build Wealth* (Brentwood, TN: The Lampo Group, Inc., 1994), 133.

4. Ramsey, *Total Money Makeover*, 34.

5. Steve Corbett and Brian Fikkert, *When Helping Hurts: How to Alleviate Poverty Without Hurting the Poor . . . and Yourself,* extended ed. (Chicago: Moody Publishers, 2012), 27.

SESSION ELEVEN: MENTORSHIP AND PARTNERING

1. Regi Campbell, *Mentor Like Jesus* (Nashville: B&H Publishing Group, 2009), 18.

2. Factors paraphrased from Bobb Biehl, "What to Look for in a Mentor," Focus on the Family website, http://www.focusonthefamily.com/marriage/strengthening_your_marriage/mentoring_101/what_to_look_for_in_a_mentor.aspx.

3. Ibid.

SESSION TWELVE: A LIFE OF GIVING IS A LIFE WORTH LIVING

1. Richard Stearns, *The Hole in Our Gospel* (Nashville: Thomas Nelson, 2010), 109.

2. Jim Elliot, as quoted in Stearns, *The Hole in Our Gospel*, 82.

ABOUT THE AUTHOR

TERRY FELBER is an author and entrepreneur who speaks to large audiences around the world about principles for successful living. He has served on the board of directors of the National Association of Evangelicals; the advisory board of Alticor, an international multibillion-dollar corporation; and a half dozen other corporate and ministry boards. He and his wife, Linda, reside in Florida.

DAVE RAMSEY is America's trusted voice on money and business. He has authored three *New York Times* bestselling books: *Financial Peace*, *More Than Enough*, and *The Total Money Makeover*. His latest book, *EntreLeadership*, was released in 2011. The *Dave Ramsey Show* is heard by more than 4.5 million listeners each week on more than five hundred radio stations. Follow Dave on Twitter (@DaveRamsey) and on the Web at daveramsey.com.

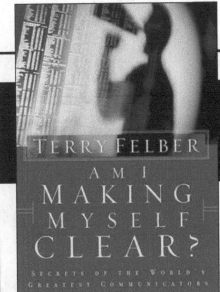

Am I Making Myself Clear?
Secrets of the World's Greatest Communicators

Lincoln, Churchill, Mother Teresa, Gutenberg—all of these individuals had something in common beyond their passion, determination, and faith: they had a remarkable grasp of the art of communication. Lack of communication is the number one reason for broken marriages, failed partnerships, and severed relationships.

In *Am I Making Myself Clear?* Terry Felber shares ten essential skills that anyone can develop and use to go beyond talking to effective communication. They include: The Art of Unspoken Language, The Art of Valuing Others, The Art of Authenticity, and The Art of Self-Talk. Felber equips readers to master all forms of communication, from participating in a simple conversation to facilitating a business meeting. For anyone interested in self-improvement and empowerment, this book is a vital resource.

SPEECHES AND SEMINARS

Terry Felber is available for
speaking engagements.
Email him at terry.felber@usa.net
for more information.

9 781400 339655